◆ ANCIENT WORLD LEADERS ◆

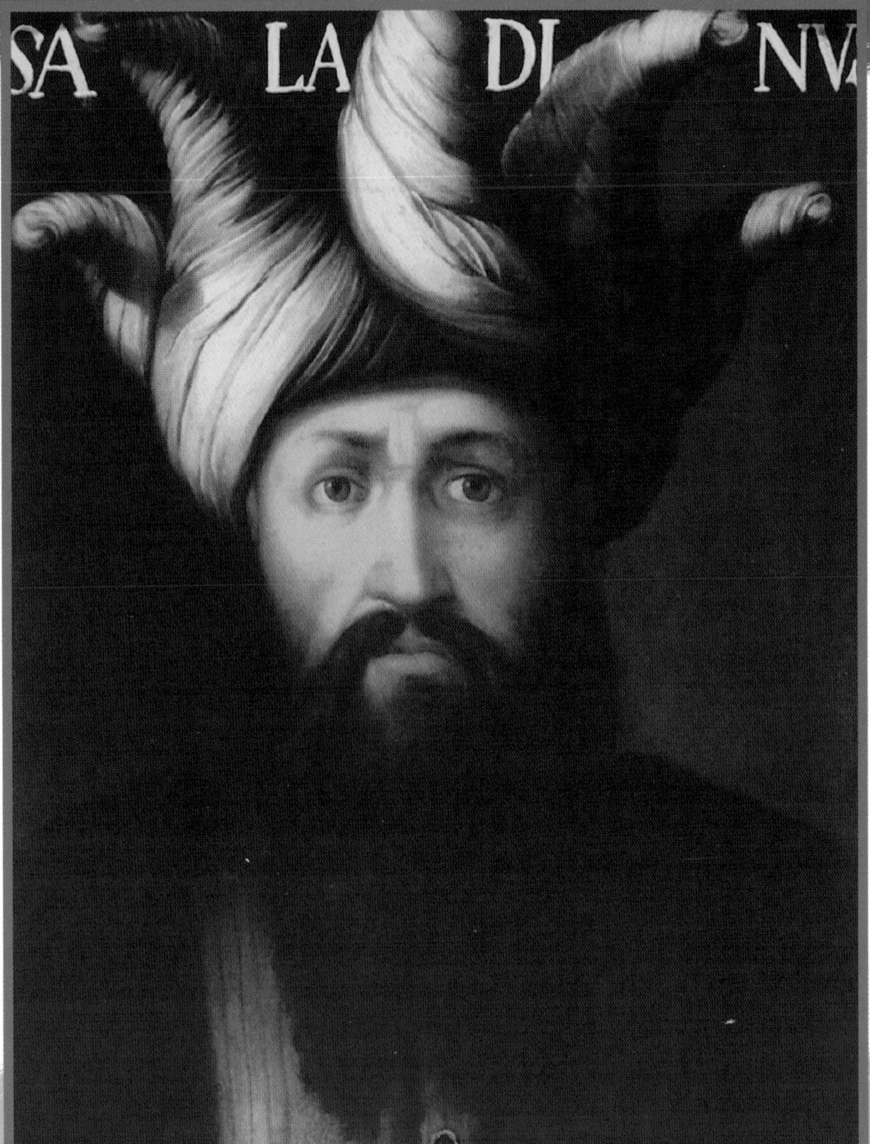
SA LA DI NV

◆ ANCIENT WORLD LEADERS ◆

SALADIN

◆◆◆

John Davenport

CHELSEA HOUSE
PUBLISHERS
A Haights Cross Communications ◆ Company

Philadelphia

Frontispiece: A portrait of Saladin, the Kurdish sultan of Egypt and Syria who would go on to be one of the greatest Muslim leaders of all time.

CHELSEA HOUSE PUBLISHERS

VP, NEW PRODUCT DEVELOPMENT Sally Cheney
DIRECTOR OF PRODUCTION Kim Shinners
CREATIVE MANAGER Takeshi Takahashi
MANUFACTURING MANAGER Diann Grasse

Staff for SALADIN

ASSOCIATE EDITOR Benjamin Xavier Kim
PRODUCTION EDITOR Jaimie Winkler
PICTURE RESEARCHER Pat Holl
SERIES DESIGNER Takeshi Takahashi
COVER DESIGNER Takeshi Takahashi
LAYOUT 21st Century Publishing and Communications, Inc.

A Haights Cross Communications ⌁ Company

http://www.chelseahouse.com

First Printing

1 3 5 7 9 8 6 4 2

Library of Congress Cataloging-in-Publication Data

Davenport, John C., 1960–
    Saladin / John Davenport.
        p. cm.—(Ancient world leaders)
Includes index.
Summary: Examines the life of the very powerful and influential Muslim sultan, Saladin, who led his people in an attempt to regain holy lands in and around Jerusalem that had been lost during earlier Crusades.
    ISBN 0-7910-7223-1
    1. Saladin, Sultan of Egypt and Syria, 1137–1193—Juvenile literature. 2. Egypt—Kings and rulers—Biography—Juvenile literature. 3. Syria—Kings and rulers—Biography—Juvenile literature. 4. Crusades—Juvenile literature. [1. Saladin, Sultan of Egypt and Syria, 1137–1193. 2. Kings, queens, rulers, etc. 3. Crusades. 4. Christianity—Relations—Islam—History—To 1500. 5. Islam—Relations—Christianity—History—To 1500.] I. Title. II. Series.
DS38.4.S2 D285 2002
956'.014'092 dc21
                                                                        2002014874

◆ TABLE OF CONTENTS ◆

ON LEADERSHIP

Arthur M. Schlesinger, jr.

L eadership, it may be said, is really what makes the world go round. Love no doubt smoothes the passage; but love is a private transaction between consenting adults. Leadership is a public transaction with history. The idea of leadership affirms the capacity of individuals to move, inspire, and mobilize masses of people so that they act together in pursuit of an end. Sometimes leadership serves good purposes, sometimes bad; but whether the end is benign or evil, great leaders are those men and women who leave their personal stamp on history.

Now, the very concept of leadership implies the proposition that individuals can make a difference. This proposition has never been universally accepted. From classical times to the present day, eminent thinkers have regarded individuals as no more than the agents and pawns of larger forces, whether the gods and goddesses of the ancient world or, in the modern era, race, class, nation, the dialectic, the will of the people, the spirit of the times, history itself. Against such forces, the individual dwindles into insignificance.

So contends the thesis of historical determinism. Tolstoy's great novel *War and Peace* offers a famous statement of the case. Why, Tolstoy asked, did millions of men in the Napoleonic Wars, denying their human feelings and their common sense, move back and forth across Europe slaughtering their fellows? "The war," Tolstoy answered, "was bound to happen simply because it was bound to happen." All prior history determined it. As for leaders, they, Tolstoy said, "are but the labels that serve to give a name to an end and, like labels, they have the least possible connection with the event." The greater the leader, "the more conspicuous the inevitability and the predestination of every act he commits." The leader, said Tolstoy, is "the slave of history."

Determinism takes many forms. Marxism is the determinism of class. Nazism the determinism of race. But the idea of men and women as the slaves of history runs athwart the deepest human instincts. Rigid determinism abolishes the idea of human freedom—the assumption of free choice that underlies every move we make, every word we speak, every thought we think. It abolishes the idea of human responsibility, since it is manifestly unfair to reward or punish people for actions that are by definition beyond their control. No one can live consistently by any deterministic creed. The Marxist states prove this themselves by their extreme susceptibility to the cult of leadership.

More than that, history refutes the idea that individuals make no difference. In December 1931 a British politician crossing Fifth Avenue in New York City between 76th and 77th Streets around 10:30 P.M. looked in the wrong direction and was knocked down by an automobile— a moment, he later recalled, of a man aghast, a world aglare: "I do not understand why I was not broken like an eggshell or squashed like a gooseberry." Fourteen months later an American politician, sitting in an open car in Miami, Florida, was fired on by an assassin; the man beside him was hit. Those who believe that individuals make no difference to history might well ponder whether the next two decades would have been the same had Mario Constasino's car killed Winston Churchill in 1931 and Giuseppe Zangara's bullet killed Franklin Roosevelt in 1933. Suppose, in addition, that Lenin had died of typhus in Siberia in 1895 and that Hitler had been killed on the western front in 1916. What would the 20th century have looked like now?

For better or for worse, individuals do make a difference. "The notion that a people can run itself and its affairs anonymously," wrote the philosopher William James, "is now well known to be the silliest of absurdities. Mankind does nothing save through initiatives on the part of inventors, great or small, and imitation by the rest of us—these are the sole factors in human progress. Individuals of genius show the way, and set the patterns, which common people then adopt and follow."

Leadership, James suggests, means leadership in thought as well as in action. In the long run, leaders in thought may well make the greater difference to the world. "The ideas of economists and political philosophers, both when they are right and when they are wrong," wrote John Maynard Keynes, "are more powerful than is commonly understood. Indeed the world is ruled by little else. Practical men, who believe themselves to be quite exempt from any intellectual influences, are usually the slaves of some defunct economist. . . . The power of vested interests is vastly exaggerated compared with the gradual encroachment of ideas."

But, as Woodrow Wilson once said, "Those only are leaders of men, in the general eye, who lead in action. . . . It is at their hands that new thought gets its translation into the crude language of deeds." Leaders in thought often invent in solitude and obscurity, leaving to later generations the tasks of imitation. Leaders in action—the leaders portrayed in this series—have to be effective in their own time.

And they cannot be effective by themselves. They must act in response to the rhythms of their age. Their genius must be adapted, in a phrase from William James, "to the receptivities of the moment." Leaders are useless without followers. "There goes the mob," said the French politician, hearing a clamor in the streets. "I am their leader. I must follow them." Great leaders turn the inchoate emotions of the mob to purposes of their own. They seize on the opportunities of their time, the hopes, fears, frustrations, crises, potentialities. They succeed when events have prepared the way for them, when the community is awaiting to be aroused, when they can provide the clarifying and organizing ideas. Leadership completes the circuit between the individual and the mass and thereby alters history.

It may alter history for better or for worse. Leaders have been responsible for the most extravagant follies and most monstrous crimes that have beset suffering humanity. They have also been vital in such gains as humanity has made in individual freedom, religious and racial tolerance, social justice, and respect for human rights.

There is no sure way to tell in advance who is going to lead for good and who for evil. But a glance at the gallery of men and women in ANCIENT WORLD LEADERS suggests some useful tests.

One test is this: Do leaders lead by force or by persuasion? By command or by consent? Through most of history leadership was exercised by the divine right of authority. The duty of followers was to defer and to obey. "Theirs not to reason why/Theirs but to do and die." On occasion, as with the so-called enlightened despots of the 18th century in Europe, absolutist leadership was animated by humane purposes. More often, absolutism nourished the passion for domination, land, gold, and conquest and resulted in tyranny.

The great revolution of modern times has been the revolution of equality. "Perhaps no form of government," wrote the British historian James Bryce in his study of the United States, *The American Commonwealth,* "needs great leaders so much as democracy." The idea that all people should be equal in their legal condition has undermined the old structure of authority, hierarchy, and deference. The revolution of equality has had two contrary effects on the nature of leadership. For equality, as Alexis de Tocqueville pointed out in his great study *Democracy in America,* might mean equality in servitude as well as equality in freedom.

"I know of only two methods of establishing equality in the political world," Tocqueville wrote. "Rights must be given to every citizen, or none at all to anyone . . . save one, who is the master of all." There was no middle ground "between the sovereignty of all and the absolute power of one man." In his astonishing prediction of 20th-century totalitarian dictatorship, Tocqueville explained how the revolution of equality could lead to the *Führerprinzip* and more terrible absolutism than the world had ever known.

But when rights are given to every citizen and the sovereignty of all is established, the problem of leadership takes a new form, becomes more exacting than ever before. It is easy to issue commands and enforce them by the rope and the stake, the concentration camp and the *gulag.* It is much harder to use argument and achievement to overcome opposition and win consent. The Founding Fathers of the United States understood the difficulty. They believed that history had given them the opportunity to decide, as Alexander Hamilton wrote in the first Federalist Paper, whether men are indeed capable of basing government on "reflection and choice, or whether they are forever destined to depend . . . on accident and force."

Government by reflection and choice called for a new style of leadership and a new quality of followership. It required leaders to be responsive to popular concerns, and it required followers to be active and informed participants in the process. Democracy does not eliminate emotion from politics; sometimes it fosters demagoguery; but it is confident that, as the greatest of democratic leaders put it, you cannot fool all of the people all of the time. It measures leadership by results and retires those who overreach or falter or fail.

It is true that in the long run despots are measured by results too. But they can postpone the day of judgment, sometimes indefinitely, and in the meantime they can do infinite harm. It is also true that democracy is no guarantee of virtue and intelligence in government, for the voice of the people is not necessarily the voice of God. But democracy, by assuring the right of opposition, offers built-in resistance to the evils inherent in absolutism. As the theologian Reinhold Niebuhr summed it up, "Man's capacity for justice makes democracy possible, but man's inclination to justice makes democracy necessary."

A second test for leadership is the end for which power is sought. When leaders have as their goal the supremacy of a master race or the promotion of totalitarian revolution or the acquisition and exploitation of colonies or the protection of greed and privilege or the preservation of personal power, it is likely that their leadership will do little to advance the cause of humanity. When their goal is the abolition of slavery, the liberation of women, the enlargement of opportunity for the poor and powerless, the extension of equal rights to racial minorities, the defense of the freedoms of expression and opposition, it is likely that their leadership will increase the sum of human liberty and welfare.

Leaders have done great harm to the world. They have also conferred great benefits. You will find both sorts in this series. Even "good" leaders must be regarded with a certain wariness. Leaders are not demigods; they put on their trousers one leg after another just like ordinary mortals. No leader is infallible, and every leader needs to be reminded of this at regular intervals. Irreverence irritates leaders but is their salvation. Unquestioning submission corrupts leaders and demeans followers. Making a cult of a leader is always a mistake. Fortunately hero worship generates its own antidote. "Every hero," said Emerson, "becomes a bore at last."

The single benefit the great leaders confer is to embolden the rest of us to live according to our own best selves, to be active, insistent, and resolute in affirming our own sense of things. For great leaders attest to the reality of human freedom against the supposed inevitabilities of history. And they attest to the wisdom and power that may lie within the most unlikely of us, which is why Abraham Lincoln remains the supreme example of great leadership. A great leader, said Emerson, exhibits new possibilities to all humanity. "We feed on genius . . . . Great men exist that there may be greater men."

Great leaders, in short, justify themselves by emancipating and empowering their followers. So humanity struggles to master its destiny, remembering with Alexis de Tocqueville: "It is true that around every man a fatal circle is traced beyond which he cannot pass; but within the wide verge of that circle he is powerful and free; as it is with man, so with communities." ■

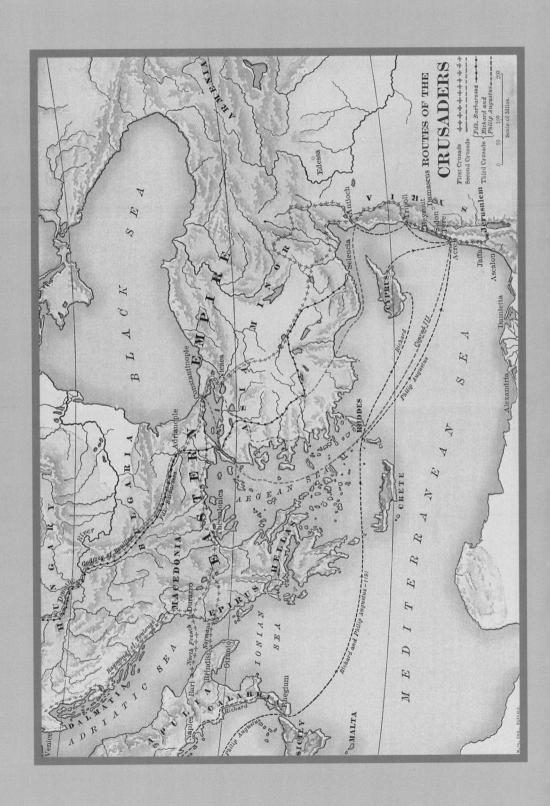

ROUTES OF THE
CRUSADERS

First Crusade +++++++++
Second Crusade ———
Fredk. Barbarossa ·-·-·-·
Third Crusade { *Richard and*
{ *Philip Augustus* ----------

Scale of Miles
0   50   100   150   200

MEDITERRANEAN SEA

A TALE
OF TWO
CONQUESTS

JERUSALEM, 1099

They sweltered. Nothing they knew from Europe could compare to the oppressive, unrelenting heat of Palestine in summer. Burdened with massive swords, battle-axes, and spears, covered in heavy chain-mail tunics, the soldiers trudged across rocky, barren ground punctuated by tawny-colored villages and dusty towns. Each drop of sweat that fell from under their conical steel helmets made their thirst greater. Their parched throats were matched only by their throbbing heads. Only here and there did some form of greenery serve as a telltale sign of precious water. From throughout western Europe, these metal-covered men had come to fight for their God. Their religious zeal burned as hotly as the ground under their feet.

Jerusalem must have seemed miragelike in its splendor. The city's trees, gardens, and orchards spoke of refreshment, while its

PIERRE L'HERMITE
1095

LOUIS VI DIT LE GROS
de 1108 à 1137

The First Crusade took place from 1096 to 1099, culminating in the conquest of Jerusalem by the European crusaders. This set the stage for years of conflict between the Christians of the West and the Muslims of the East, a situation into which Saladin would be born.

brilliant white buildings appeared heavenly as they shimmered through the waves of heat rising up among the ranks of crusaders. To be sure, these were no idle tourists or common pilgrims who now gazed upon the holiest city in the medieval world; these men were crusaders, Christian warriors. They had marched for months not to stand in awe of Jerusalem's beauty, but rather to smash its walls and kill the Muslims who held the city in the name of Islam.

Under a broiling sun, the crusader commanders viewed the battlements. Godfrey of Bouillon and Raymond of Saint-Gilles pondered the best way to crack the tough shell of walls that rose before them. Godfrey and Raymond had led their men here, and now it was up to them to organize the assault. Each man hoped that it would be a short siege. Keeping men in the field in the eleventh century was no mean feat. Steady streams of food, water, and other supplies could not always be counted upon. The men might become frustrated and dispirited; they might even go home. The walls of Jerusalem had to fall quickly.

So, the preparations began. The crusaders gathered wood and constructed huge towers that could be rolled up to the walls to disgorge fighting men over the top and into the city. They built immense, slingshot-like catapults called *mangonels*. Each one of these wooden monsters could hurl a projectile with the capacity to shatter sturdy buildings and thick ramparts. Most importantly, the warriors searched out sources of water—wells that had been neither poisoned nor filled in by the Muslims as they retreated inside Jerusalem's gates. Once the weapons had been built and their men watered, Godfrey and Raymond unleashed a furious onslaught.

On July 15, 1099, despite a rain of arrows and burning oil that poured down on their heads, the crusader army cleared Jerusalem's walls of their stubborn defenders. As the enraged attackers entered the city, Muslim and Jewish inhabitants ran for their lives toward their temples and mosques. Elderly scholars stumbled along in the panicky crowd carrying their religious books and sacred texts. Women with babies in their arms and children by the hand dashed for safety. Men prayed to Allah before what they knew would be their certain deaths. Soon, holy places burned and entire neighborhoods, filled with innocent people, fell under the mighty blows of Christian swords. The noise of battle echoed through the narrow streets of Jerusalem. Clanging armor and rattling swords drowned out every sound except for the terrified screams of people cut down where they stood. Down twisting streets and alleys, the dull clatter of horses, hooves mingled with cries of victory and defeat as the European knights slashed their way through the ancient city.

Where Jesus once walked, spreading his message of peace and love, one Christian warrior proudly remarked that "the slaughter was so great that our men waded in blood up to their ankles." In some parts of the city, Christian soldiers cut open the bodies of their Muslim victims to see if they had hidden any gold by swallowing it. In other sections, Jews were herded into their synagogues and burned alive. Near the very spot where Jesus had prayed before his crucifixion, it was said that the crusaders murdered 10,000 people.

As they finished killing, the bloodied, exhausted soldiers stepped back to view the product of their labor. Jerusalem's 40,000 Muslims and Jews lay dead, hacked apart by soldiers of God who had traveled a thousand miles to "rescue" the Holy Land. Instead, they destroyed the jewel that stood at its center. Sacred to the world's three great monotheistic religions, Jerusalem, according to a priest who accompanied the crusaders, "was filled with corpses and blood." Even before the sound of the last screams faded, the weary knights staggered into the Church of the Holy Sepulcher, reputedly built directly above Jesus' tomb, and thanked their God for victory. Jerusalem was now safe from the insult of Muslim occupation.

JERUSALEM, 1187

Ascalon, the recently conquered gateway to Egypt, seemed like a dream come true and Jerusalem only a shining possibility to the Muslim warriors. The ancient city, where it was believed that Muhammad once stepped up into heaven to converse with Moses and Jesus, called to the men across the dusty plains and craggy hills of Palestine. Soldiers of all descriptions marched excitedly toward their priceless objective. Riding proudly in the vanguard of the army were the horse archers with their short, powerful bows. These *mamluks*, as they were called, made up the elite of the Muslim force. Lightly armored, the mamluks rode swift horses bedecked with colorful ribbons and occasionally armored blankets. In amongst these warriors rode other cavalrymen carrying spears and javelins. All of the soldiers carried swords; many wielded the infamous curved sabers reportedly capable of slicing a man's arm off with a single stroke. Behind the riders, the infantry marched in long columns. When it came time to lay siege to Jerusalem, the infantry would swing into action. With their axes, spears, and crossbows they would surround the city and protect the Syrian engineers whose job it was to dig under and weaken Jerusalem's walls to the point of collapse. If required, special infantrymen could be called upon to throw incendiary grenades filled with a flammable liquid known as *naphtha* at their enemies. It was indeed a formidable army, and for each man in it, Jerusalem meant victory. They looked forward to plundering its riches, but they also hungered for revenge. Blood for blood, the Muslim fighters pledged themselves to a holy war, a war to recapture Jerusalem and drive out the Christian infidels who defiled the land of Muhammad.

Finally, they reached their goal. Taking up positions to the west of a frightened but defiant city, they prepared to lay siege. The army's commander had given Jerusalem's Christian leaders an opportunity to surrender without a fight, and thereby avoid a massacre, before the Muslim forces had even left their camp at Ascalon. He offered very generous terms—so generous, in fact, that some of the commander's captains argued strenuously that he was being too lenient toward such vile unbelievers. But it didn't matter, for Jerusalem's emissaries rejected all of the terms. Instead, the city mustered what fighting men it could and boldly offered battle.

The contest that followed raged for five long weeks. The tenacity and courage of Jerusalem's defenders surprised their opponents, while the persistence of the attacking Muslims worried their counterparts manning the walls. Then, suddenly, the Muslim commander disengaged his troops and began to move north. Some in Jerusalem thought he was running away, but the man directing the defense knew better; the Muslims were only shifting their position. They had been trying to force their way over rocky terrain, uphill, against the strongest part of Jerusalem's walls. Realizing this, the Muslim commander was now swinging his forces around to the exact spot taken by Godfrey and Raymond 88 years earlier. Using the cross that had been erected in Godfrey's honor as a rallying point, the sultan now launched his fiercest assault.

Engineers from Syria moved forward under the cover of shields and dug holes under the walls. Once they completed the tunnels, they propped up the huge stones with wooden supports. The workers then set the supports on fire, moved a safe distance away, and waited for them to burn through and the walls to come crashing to the ground. As they did, Muslim warriors poured through the breach and, in the face of desperate opposition, fought their way into the Holy City. The flags and banners of Islam once again fluttered over Jerusalem.

Now the slaughter should have begun. Tradition held that unpaid, infuriated soldiers had the right to plunder a city if it had been taken by storm. The unfortunate occupants of such a prize had no right to live and could be murdered at will. The Muslims had offered terms and they had been insolently rejected. As a result, the conquerors, exhausted by more resolute resistance than they had expected, anticipated being given a free hand to loot, rape, and kill. In any case, so the soldiers felt, this was *jihad*—a struggle against the mortal enemies of Islam—and revenge for the massacre of 1099 was rightfully theirs. No Muslim leader could deny this.

But the man who held Jerusalem's fate was no ordinary leader. He cast his thoughtful eye around the city and searched his soul. He could let his men loose or restrain them; he could harden his heart or open it to compassion. The weary commander thought ahead and considered the consequences of destroying the city. He could show mercy; what would be the implications of that? Just days before, Jerusalem's Christians prayed to God for deliverance. They fell to their knees and

Saladin commanded the 1187 conquest of Jerusalem, taking the city back from the previous inhabitants, the Christian crusaders. However, Saladin would distinguish himself from other conquerors of the Crusades by his displays of mercy—and, at times, cooperation—with his enemies.

begged Jesus to save them. Yet now their fate rested on the decision of this one man. A word from him and they either died in agony or lived in peace. Sixty thousand men, women, and children waited for a word from the greatest Muslim leader of his day—Saladin.

SALADIN'S
WORLD

Jerusalem fell in July 1099 to an army of crusaders, many of whom had
marched all the way from France to fight a holy war against Muslims
they believed to be the enemies of God. Their journey began in 1095
when, at a place called Clermont, in France, Pope Urban II called on the
nobles of Europe to expel the Muslims from the land where Christianity
had been born. Responding to a call for help from their fellow Christians
in the Byzantine Empire, the pope told the men gathered at Clermont
that the Muslim presence in the Holy Land was an affront to the
Almighty. Pope Urban begged them to consider the disgrace of having
nonbelievers in control of the very soil upon which the Son of God
himself and his apostles had trodden. "Oh, race of Franks . . . race
beloved and chosen by God," Urban bellowed, "an accursed race, a race
wholly alienated from God . . . has violently invaded the lands [of the
Eastern Christians] and has depopulated them by pillage and fire."
Through "cruel tortures," the pope screamed, the Muslims had

Pope Urban II proposed what became the First Crusade in 1095 to the nobles of Europe. In effect, his proposal was a move to dispel the growing power of the European nobles in order to maintain the Catholic Church's own power. Not only did Pope Urban II appeal to the nobles' sense of religious fervor, but also to their thirst for land and glory, which could be theirs while fighting these crusades.

"destroyed the churches of God . . . after having defiled them with their uncleanness."

As Urban spoke, the nobles listened reverently but seemed oddly unmoved until the pope made a direct plea for their services. "On whom, therefore, rests the labor of avenging these wrongs and of recovering this territory, if not upon you," Urban exclaimed, "you, upon whom, above all other nations, God has conferred remarkable glory in arms." Finally, with an accusatory eye, the pope paused to hear the nobles' reply. Seemingly with one voice, inspired by Urban's impassioned speech, the lords and barons before him cried out, "It is the will of God! It is the will of

God!" At this the pope grinned, lifted his eyes skyward, and thanked the Lord in Heaven. The First Crusade had begun.

Urban II, and the popes who would come after him over the next 175 years, had many reasons for sending waves of armored knights to conquer and occupy the area known as Palestine. To begin with, the relationship between Europe's political and religious elite, which had never been good, had soured badly in the late 11th century. The most powerful single kingdom in Europe, that of the Franks (who lived in what would become modern France), distrusted the pope and envied his power. One of their neighbors, the German king Henry IV, went so far as to challenge openly papal authority in his realm. The resulting dispute, in which the pope actually cast Henry out of the Church for a time, pitted religion directly against the state and cast a cloud of hostility over Christian Europe.

Kings and lesser nobles everywhere resented the Church's power and sought continually to reduce the pope's influence while at the same time increasing their own. Urban II saw all of this clearly and hoped that a holy war—or better yet, a series of holy wars—might distract the restless, ambitious nobility. Military campaigns in distant lands would physically remove the threat posed by the nobles—especially the younger, more rebellious ones—and give the lords of Europe something other to do than look with envy upon the Church. But temporarily getting rid of his political enemies would not really, in the long run, solve the pope's problems.

So, the deal was sweetened. Pope Urban offered those nobles willing to serve as religious warriors something called *plenary indulgence*, or forgiveness beforehand for any crimes they might commit while crusading. He also promised the soldiers that they could keep the land they captured as states of their own. They would be masters in the new lands, with all the wealth and power that entailed. By blessing the establishment of these crusader states in Palestine, Urban tied Europe's most powerful and aggressive men to him indirectly through bonds of gratitude and dependence. Land in the Middle Ages meant everything. If the land the crusaders would gain came solely as a result of their actions in the service of God, then naturally the pope, as God's representative on earth, would have nothing to fear from the nobility.

Internal politics and power struggles certainly created much of the impulse to crusade, but so did an increasing sense of unease regarding the rise of Islam—not only in terms of adherents who actually acknowledged no god but Allah and revered Muhammad as his messenger, but also in sheer geographical scope. By the middle of the 11th century, Islam covered a vast area from Spain to the frontiers of India, from Central Asia to Central Africa. In short, a huge chunk of the known world at the time followed the precepts of the Koran, the Islamic holy book that contained the word of God as dictated to Muhammad by an archangel. Among these millions of Muslims were vast numbers of warriors who, when well led, were capable of defeating almost any army. They proved this in 1071, when the Seljuk Turks, fierce horsemen from the steppes of Central Asia, overwhelmed the Byzantine army at Manzikert. The Byzantines, as the descendents of Rome's Eastern Empire, inherited Rome's military prowess. Their *cataphracts,* or armored knights, were well-known and much feared; yet the Muslim Turks swept them away in one stroke.

Perhaps more important was the fact that most of the world's major trade routes passed through Muslim lands, even if they ended up depositing their vital goods in Christian countries. This put Islam in a commanding position. By the time of the First Crusade, the political, religious, economic, and military might of Islam loomed large in the European imagination.

The victory at Manzikert put Islam in direct contact with what remained of the Byzantine Empire and, through it, Christian Western Europe. Although Christianity and Islam shared roots in the Old Testament, the two great faiths became anxious as their borders squeezed up against each other. Hope for a crucial dialogue, however, existed at this same intersection. Trade, profit,

A scene depicting the prophet Muhammad (with his face blocked out, as it is usually depicted in Islamic art) receiving the Koran, or the Islamic religious texts thought to be direct from God. However, Islam had fractured into different sects that had opposing interpretations of Islam, often resulting in infighting, as well as offering up poor resistance to outside forces, including the more unified Christian crusaders.

the natural desire for peaceful prosperity rather than conflict, and sheer curiosity under different circumstances might have drawn together these two mutually dissimilar societies. Instead, in the case of Christianity and Islam, the more contact they had with each other, the more they worried about and distrusted each other. Suspicion and intolerance became the norm.

By the time Saladin was born in 1138, the world had already become too small. Decades of accumulated tension had broken many years earlier, leading to a series of vicious Christian-Muslim wars known collectively as the Crusades. The armed contest between the followers of Christ and those of Muhammad went poorly at first for the latter. Torn by religious disagreements and ethnic differences, Muslims found themselves largely incapable of resisting the European onslaught unleashed by Urban II at Clermont. The recapture of Jerusalem in 1099 during the First Crusade (1096-1099), ending over 450 years of Muslim rule, inaugurated a long period of Christian dominance in the Holy Land. This time witnessed the creation of four independent Christian kingdoms—the Principality of Antioch, the County of Edessa, the County of Tripoli, and the powerful Kingdom of Jerusalem. These states, with their formidable armies and nearly impregnable fortresses, constantly reminded the Muslims of their own weaknesses and humiliated them.

The crusaders quickly blended into their new environs, or the *Outremer* as they called it. Most learned to speak Arabic and adopted local customs of dress, diet, and behavior; some even embraced part or all of Islam. Still, many Muslims resented their presence and wanted them gone. From the fall of Jerusalem on, one Muslim leader after another schemed and maneuvered to evict the Franks. The Second Crusade (1147–1149) was, in part, a response to such Muslim ambitions, especially in the person of the great Syrian warrior Nur al-Din, of whom more will be said later. As it turned out, however, very little effort was required of the Europeans to keep their foothold in Palestine. Despite some Muslim victories, such as the conquest of Edessa in 1144, and some Christian defeats, such as the failure to take Damascus during the Second Crusade, the European occupation seemed destined to be a permanent feature of life in Palestine.

In their fruitless struggle against the Christian invaders, the Muslims played for very high stakes. On Islam's northern flank stood the Byzantine Empire, the last remnant of the once all-powerful Roman Empire. Although separated from their western cousins by a religious split in 1054, the Byzantines were still Christians and, as such, remained hostile to Islam. Worse yet, their geographical position right up against an expanding Muslim world made them a troublesome and dangerous threat. Granted, the Byzantines, from their capital at Constantinople (modern Istanbul, Turkey), governed less and less territory as time passed, especially after the Turks began encroaching on their lands. Good Byzantine emperors, moreover, were few and far between. The empire suffered from a chronic lack of competent, aggressive leaders. Still, the Byzantine army had a little sting left in its tail and could endanger Islam's northwestern borderlands, especially if marauding Frankish crusaders to the south made their job easier.

Nothing, however, matched the destructive potential of the deep and bitter divisions within Islam itself. Since 650, several versions of Islam competed for the hearts, souls, and loyalties of the Muslim masses. While national and regional tensions troubled the Europeans routinely, these warriors at least carried with them to Palestine a single set of religious beliefs and practices, and answered to a fairly unified religious-political chain of command. Muslims, on the contrary, had been arguing for centuries about what it meant to live by the word of Allah.

Shortly after the death of Muhammad in 632, two rival interpretations of his teachings and ideas emerged. Those Muslims who claimed to follow the direct successors of Muhammad— a group of his in-laws known as the Rashidun—referred to themselves as Sunni and quickly rose to political power. The Sunni viewed Islam as a function of the Muslim community and emphasized following the teachings of the Koran as expressed by religious leaders called *caliphs* and their secular counterparts, or *sultans*. The Sunni's opponents, known as Shiites, argued that following earthly leaders and adhering strictly to custom were far less important than experiencing a deeply emotional, personal relationship with God. Like the Sunni, the Shiites followed the Koran and strictly abided by the Muslim religious laws, or *Shariah*, but they believed that only Muhammad's son-in-law and cousin, Ali ibn Talib, inaugurated a legitimate line of political and religious succession from the Prophet. Shiites also relied much more than the Sunni on spiritual guidance from learned men they called *imams.*

A third group, the Sufis, stood outside of, but often influenced, each of these mainstream brands of Islam. Sufism reflected the mystical side of the faith through its emphasis on a wholly inner experience of the divine. Standing with the Sunni and the Shiites on either side often proved dangerous for the Sufis, given the fact that the disagreements between the first two groups often exploded into factional violence and even outright civil war.

Political maneuvering among men jostling for control over the growing Muslim population worsened the Sunni-Shiite split. *Caliphates,* or religious dynasties, came and went or dragged on much longer than their lack of real power should have permitted. No matter how long they endured, caliphs chafed most of the time under the effective rule of military strongmen, the sultans. These sultans were usually much more interested in personal gain in this world than paradise in the next. The rivalries and contests, as well as the constant bickering between the sultans and their representatives—men who went by the titles of *atabeg* and *emir*—resulted in a fractured and dangerously disunited Islam. Such instability often aided the Christians in times of battle.

The European challenge was real, and what Islam needed was a leader who could bridge the broad divides that separated and weakened Muslims, while at the same time offering an effective defense against the ever-menacing crusaders. Threatened from the outside and crippled by divisions within, Islam needed an anchor—a singular man of cunning, intellect, skill, and piety who might check and perhaps even turn back the Christian tide in the Holy Land. Islam needed a warrior-sultan to do God's will and protect the community of Believers. In the end, the Muslims got both more and less than they bargained for.

3

RISE TO POWER

The Europeans called him Saladin out of respect for his intelligence and tenacity. They saw it as something of an honor for an unbeliever from a strange culture to have his name made easier for Christians to pronounce. His name at birth, however, had a more melodic ring to it—Salah al-Din Yusef ibn Ayyub. Muslim names are more than labels, though. Traditionally, names implied God's purpose for a child and gave the individual a clear moral direction and singular focus for his life. Taken together, the name translates to "Joseph, son of Ayyub, who is the well-being (or honor) of religion." Being given the task of ensuring Islam's well-being and defending its honor conferred not only great responsibility but also a certain confidence that God would guide one to victory. Saladin would surely need such a firm foundation and assurance as he set out to bring unity, security, and stability to the Muslim world.

Saladin was actually born Salah al-Din Yusef ibn Ayyub. Born in what is now Iraq, he would be led to glory as the sultan of Egypt and Syria through a path forged by his father and uncle that reflected the dynamic and dangerous nature of Islamic politics and power plays.

Born in 1138 in Tikrit, in what is today the nation of Iraq, Saladin unwillingly entered a tumultuous, conflict-ridden landscape. The war between Islam and Christian Europe still simmered, periodically boiling over into armed clashes. Perhaps worse for Saladin, he was born into the swirl and storm of medieval Islamic politics. Chaos and confusion reigned whenever the followers of Allah tried to present a united front to the followers of Christ. Muslims fought amongst themselves almost as much as they did against the crusaders. In such a hazardous place, a little Kurdish boy could get lost; Saladin would need more than an auspicious name to guide him. He needed the type of head start in life that only diligent, determined parents could give.

We know nothing of Saladin's mother; she and her influence on him are lost to history. Of his brothers and sister we know a bit more, but not much beyond the supporting roles they played in Saladin's exploits. Saladin's father, on the other hand, is where the story really begins.

Saladin's father was an ambitious Kurd by the name of Najm al-Din Ayyub who hailed from the town of Tawin in modern Armenia. His role in carving out a political niche for the as-yet-unborn Saladin began when he left his hometown with his younger brother, Shirkuh, and sought a career serving the Abbasid caliph in Baghdad. Through a friend at the caliph's court, Ayyub secured an appointment as governor of Tikrit. The governor's job was a good solid one, but it promised little chance of real advancement unless something totally unexpected happened. This unexpected event occurred when Ayyub met a rising young Muslim Turk named Imad al-Din Zengi. Zengi was an officer serving under the Seljuk sultan. When the sultan fell out with the caliph, Zengi found himself to be a hunted man. Once, while being pursued by some of the caliph's supporters, Zengi sought refuge at Tikrit. Ayyub took Zengi in and protected him. This favor angered the caliph, but it won for Ayyub Zengi's lasting gratitude.

Zengi soon got his chance to repay Ayyub's generosity. On the very night of Saladin's birth in 1138, an unforeseen turn of events forced Ayyub and Shirkuh to flee Tikrit.

Whether it was a city guard or a Christian merchant (the details are a little hazy), Shirkuh killed a man. Recalling how angry Baghdad had been over his assistance to Zengi, Ayyub knew that the caliph would not help him save Shirkuh from being prosecuted for murder. So, the two brothers slipped out of Tikrit and made their way to Mosul, where Zengi had risen to become the *atabeg,* or local ruler. Zengi's fame had grown since he last saw Ayyub. His new-found glory put him in a position to welcome Ayyub and Shirkuh warmly. More importantly, Zengi needed trust-worthy men around him, so he quickly offered Ayyub a job in his government. Zengi gave Saladin's father command of the strategic city of Baalbek.

Fate took another turn in 1146. A slave stabbed Zengi to death. The assassination created a power vacuum that was only partially filled by Zengi's son, Mahmud, better known as Nur al-Din. Zengi's death left Ayyub in a tight spot. Shirkuh quickly took a command under Nur al-Din, but Ayyub lacked the military capability and political influence to protect his exposed position at Baalbek. As a result, when troops from the independent city of Damascus attacked Baalbek, Ayyub had to surrender. This allied him, however unintentionally, with Nur al-Din's opponents—and thus set him against his own brother. Ayyub's political senses told him that no matter how difficult such an arrangement might become, now was not a good time for heroics; he would have to take sides against Nur al-Din, at least temporarily. Ayyub's new bosses rewarded his realistic thinking with land, a confirmation of his leadership at Baalbek, and an appoint-ment as commander of Damascus's militia. The young Saladin could now prepare himself for the future from a position of relative privilege.

Saladin watched his father and learned the lessons needed to survive and advance in the rough-and-tumble Muslim political world where assassination and rebellion

The city of Damascus would be an important one for Saladin's development as a leader. His father commanded the militia in Damascus. Later, Saladin would march upon Damascus to become vizier after the death of his uncle, and later would claim the title of regent for Nur al-Din's young son.

were accepted tools for upward career mobility. From his tutors, Saladin learned the details of Arab history, a subject he studied with a passion. The precocious boy memorized not only the genealogies of famous Muslim leaders, but also the bloodlines of their horses! Above everything else, Saladin immersed himself in religion. Like all Muslim boys his age, Saladin conscientiously read the Koran, memorizing entire passages.

He even analyzed the ongoing dispute between the Sunni and Shiite sects of Islam. Although a devout Sunni, Saladin sympathized with the Shiite minority and found their emphasis on a personal relationship with God intriguing, and even a little bit alluring. He absorbed some Shiite ideas and took in some Sufism as well. Saladin was always somewhat on the emotional side and never failed to express his feelings openly and unashamedly. Sufism's focus on introspection and emotion, as a result, meshed well with him.

Another form of schooling began for Saladin at age 14. Ayyub sent his teenage son to the city of Aleppo. There he was to learn the military lessons that only his uncle Shirkuh could teach. Shirkuh, a short, one-eyed, heavy bear of a man, was the family fighter. He took Saladin hunting and taught him how to ride and kill. After the boy mastered these skills, Shirkuh taught lessons in dispatching another kind of prey. "Hold it tight under your arm," Shirkuh would bark as Saladin practiced with the traditional cavalry weapon, the lance. "Don't wave it about!" Similar instruction followed in archery and swordplay. Over time, Saladin grew skilled in the art of war. He learned from Shirkuh how to harden himself for battle and prepare for the trials of leadership.

In 1156, Saladin returned to Damascus, where his father had surrendered to Nur al-Din two years before. Now he was a man in his own right at the age of 18. His military and political training had been second to none, and now he was firmly established at the court of Islam's most influential ruler. The future greeted Saladin and awaited only his energy and ambition to carry the young man forward.

SALADIN IN EGYPT

Fatimid Egypt emerged out of the wreckage of the Abbasid dynasty. Beginning around the year 900, the Abbasids, who had ruled the Muslim Near East for almost a century and a half, watched as their power declined and the various parts of the empire they controlled went their separate ways. Egypt was one of those parts. The Egyptians formed their own caliphate, separate from the one that already existed in Baghdad, supported by its own government and army. Since the caliph in Cairo traced the line of his authority back to Muhammad's daughter, Fatima, his realm became known as Fatimid Egypt. Due to the fact that Fatima's husband, Ali, was recognized by the Shiites as the sole legitimate heir to the Prophet, Fatimid Egypt became a Shiite stronghold that blatantly defied the Sunni caliph and the sultans allied with him.

For two centuries, Fatimid Egypt grew and prospered. But by the mid-12th century, all was not well along the banks of the Nile. Tensions similar to those between the sultan and caliph in Syria had grown between al-Adid, the caliph in Cairo, and a cunning politician named Shawar. Looking for nothing less than complete control over Egypt, Shawar demanded that al-Adid make him the *vizier,* or chief government official. Yet many men coveted such an important post. Shawar needed a strong patron to support his quest. Lacking the power necessary to force al-Adid to appoint him, Shawar solicited help from abroad in his struggle at home. Naturally he turned to Syria and Nur al-Din—who, for his part, wanted more influence over affairs in the eastern Mediterranean, and knew that the caliph would be in his debt if he succeeded in nudging Shiite Egypt back into the Sunni fold. After some thought, Nur al-Din agreed and promised Syrian troops to Shawar. The soldiers would serve under Shirkuh and his 26-year-old nephew, Saladin. Just as Shawar had hoped, the appearance of such a mighty expeditionary force

as that commanded by Shirkuh prompted the Fatimid
caliph to appoint Shawar as vizier. Once in power, however,
Shawar became nervous with so many armed Syrians in
Egypt; he quickly made it clear that he wanted them to go
home. Shirkuh and Saladin, however, were not so keen to
leave without explicit orders to do so from Damascus, and
stayed put.

Shawar feared the Syrians, and knew just how vulnerable
Egypt was. He also realized what an attractive target Egypt
presented to other parties, namely the Byzantines and
Franks. The new vizier could not fight all these enemies, nor
could he ally Egypt with both Christians and Muslims at the
same time. Shawar's dilemma forced him to consider which
of his possible adversaries represented the greatest threat
to his position and the independence of Egypt. Compelled
to choose the lesser of these evils, Shawar sent word to
Jerusalem that he wanted to talk to the Franks. In the end,
the vizier feared Nur al-Din more than anyone else, so he
invited the king of Jerusalem, Amalric, to form an alliance.
Amalric might come and go, if the right price could be
found, but Nur al-Din threatened Shawar's very basis for
control. Amalric, additionally, was no Shirkuh, and he most
certainly had no second in command to match Saladin.
Shawar figured that Amalric could be handled far more easily
than the Syrians could.

Open warfare between the Fatimid-Frankish army and
the Syrians now erupted. In their first engagement, Shirkuh
and Saladin quickly put their opponents on the run, proving
the superiority of Syrian arms and tactics. But instead of
following up his rout of the enemy with a vigorous pursuit,
Shirkuh fell back into Lower Egypt to protect his lines of
supply and communication centered on the city of Alexandria.
Once Shirkuh arrived, he gave the job of protecting the city
over to Saladin. During the siege that followed, Saladin
managed the defenses splendidly. Although the garrison

A Fatimid illustration of two horsemen in combat. The Fatimid warriors, under the leadership of the vizier Shawar, aligned themselves with the Christian Franks and fought with the Syrians, with whom Saladin and his uncle Shirkuh fought.

suffered greatly from hunger and thirst and struggled to hold the Franks at bay, the city held out long enough for Nur al-Din to distract Amalric by attacking northern Palestine. Jerusalem's king, fearing that his base of power might fall while he sat outside of Alexandria, had no choice but to ask Saladin for a truce. Victorious but weakened by the long siege, Saladin needed to return home to Syria for reinforcements, so he gladly accepted the Frankish offer. Saladin had won, but the experience left a lasting impression on him and gave the future sultan a lifelong aversion to siege warfare. Later, Saladin remarked that fighting and privation in Egypt changed him forever. "I suffered such hardships at Alexandria," he once told a friend, "as I shall never forget."

With the siege behind him, Saladin marched back to Damascus. No sooner had he settled in, however, then news arrived of a new Frankish invasion of Egypt. Shirkuh's best chance to set matters straight in Egypt had come at last. "Yusef," Shirkuh shouted at Saladin, "pack your things! We're going!" Although he loathed the idea of going back, Saladin joined Shirkuh and returned once again. This time, the Franks pulled out before the Syrians even arrived, leaving Shawar without his Christian allies. Now came the moment for Shirkuh to break the scheming vizier once and for all. Soon after arriving, Saladin and some of his troops caught Shawar riding near the Great Pyramids and promptly killed him. The frightened caliph immediately elevated Shirkuh to Shawar's office. Saladin's uncle, for all intents and purposes, now ruled Egypt.

Shirkuh, however brave, had his faults. One was a tendency to overeat. As a matter of fact, Shirkuh loved to gorge himself at banquets. This habit proved fateful for Saladin. After one particularly huge meal, Shirkuh fell ill and suddenly died. Once again, Egypt was adrift. Who would become the vizier now? Saladin was the name on everyone's lips. Bright and competent, Shirkuh's nephew seemed to be the logical choice. First, the Syrian emirs discussed the matter and decided that Saladin would make a fine leader. Next, the caliph in Cairo had to make up his mind. He knew very little about Saladin other than his exploits at Alexandria and his fine service to Shirkuh, so he turned to his advisers. They convinced the caliph that he could easily dominate the young man. "There is no one weaker," they said, "than Yusef [Saladin]." In a singular act of underestimation, al-Adid chose to elevate Saladin into his uncle's position. Saladin accepted and took the title Al-Malik al-Nasir, "the victorious king."

Back in Damascus, Nur al-Din publicly congratulated Saladin, but privately he worried that Saladin might not remain an obedient vassal. As time passed, relations between the two men became strained. Saladin, sensing the tension, accelerated his consolidation of power in Egypt. He moved quickly to destroy the Fatimid army and undermine the caliph. Saladin had just begun to implement his scheme when suddenly fate intervened on Saladin's behalf as it would so often in the future; in 1171, al-Adid died unexpectedly.

Free now to do as he pleased, Saladin reconstituted the Egyptian army around a Syrian core and made certain that the new force gave its loyalty to him exclusively rather than to Nur al-Din, as people had expected. Saladin then proceeded to strengthen his position by currying favor with the Abbasid caliph directly, making an end run around Nur al-Din. In a clear effort to win the caliph's heart, Saladin officially reinstated the Sunni faith in Egypt. Feeling intensely suspicious and very threatened, Nur al-Din prepared in the spring of 1174 to rein in his young protégé by force. He put together an army and readied an expedition designed to punish Saladin and put Egypt back under his control. But, once again, God appeared to shine on Saladin—Nur al-Din died before leaving Syria.

Saladin's time had arrived. Nur al-Din had made the mistake of leaving his empire in the hands of a son too young to rule in his own right. A struggle ensued to determine who would serve as regent for the boy. Saladin saw his chance and grabbed it. He threw together a small force of about 700 trusted men and set out for Damascus. Before he left, Saladin declared his loyalty to Nur al-Din's son, but really he wanted power for himself. Marching unopposed to Damascus, Saladin occupied the city and claimed the regent's title. Most of Nur al-Din's cities rejected Saladin's claim, but the caliph in Baghdad, feeling grateful for the return of Egypt, somewhat reluctantly recognized Saladin and proclaimed him to be the Sultan of Syria and Egypt. The son of Ayyub was now the master, even if in name only, of the Muslim Near East.

THE
SULTAN

UNIFYING ISLAM

Serious challenges and obstacles faced Saladin as he assumed power in Syria in 1174. To begin with, Saladin immediately came into conflict with Nur al-Din's relatives, who controlled key cities in his new domain. Chief among these cities, most of which would soon cause Saladin a great deal of trouble, were Mosul and Aleppo. At Mosul, Nur al-Din's nephew, Saif al-Din Ghazi, reigned supreme; the deceased sultan's other nephew, Imad al-Din, held the strategic city of Sinjar. Most importantly, Nur al-Din had left the crucial fortress at Aleppo in the hands of his young son Al-Malik al-Salih Ismail. Saladin needed to win these rulers over to his side or force them into submission. As it turned out, he had to do things the hard way; war between fellow Muslims became inevitable.

Saladin viewed his contest with the last of the Zengid rulers in terms of his overall plan for holy war against the Franks. For

Aleppo was one of two Muslim cities that openly defied Saladin's leadership. Soon Saladin would attack Aleppo and fight against a combined Muslim army of fighters from Aleppo and Mosul, the other city that did not recognize Saladin's position.

instance, after his capture of the city of Homs, a critical stronghold that openly refused to acknowledge his authority, Saladin justified killing other Muslims by accusing them of obstructing the course of the coming jihad. Saladin regretted shedding his fellow Muslims' blood, but he claimed to have no other choice. Saladin knew that the Koran warned that any Muslim who killed a fellow Believer "intentionally will be cast into Hell," but it also commanded that Muslim rebels be fought "till sedition comes to an end" (Koran, 4:93; 2:193). So Saladin assured his followers that "our move was not made in order to snatch a kingdom for ourselves," but rather "to set up the standards of Holy War." His opponents at Homs, he continued, "had become enemies, preventing the accomplishment of our purpose with regard to the war" against the Christians. The rebellious cities, according to Saladin, obstructed the path of holy war and, as the Koran said, those who do not "fight in the way of God . . . only fight for the power of evil" (Koran, 4:76).

Saladin's task at Homs was nothing compared to the ones he would face at Mosul and Aleppo. These two powerful cities mocked Saladin with their open defiance and denial of his claim to leadership until Saladin finally took the initiative and laid siege to Aleppo. Recognizing a mutual threat and a showdown when they saw one, the Mosulis and Aleppans joined forces and put an army in the field against Saladin's troops. The two Muslim armies met in battle on April 13, 1175, and Saladin soon proved his skills as a commander. After intense fighting, the Mosuli-Aleppan army fell in defeat and threw itself on Saladin's mercy. The sultan, at this point, revealed the side of his personality that so impressed friend and foe alike during his lifetime. Rather than making an example out of the prisoners he captured by publicly executing them, Saladin showed great restraint. He sent orders to his men that no wounded prisoners were to be killed and there would be no pursuit of enemy warriors who fled the battlefield. Those able-bodied men taken captive were to be released, and, above all, Saladin gave strict orders that no general slaughter would be tolerated, as one might expect after a medieval military action. Saladin no doubt remembered that the Koran told Muslims to "cease to be hostile" when rebels came to their senses (Koran, 2:193). Mosul and Aleppo had been brought to heel through violence, so hard feelings could not be totally avoided, but Saladin wanted as few as possible. He needed a united Islam, one without the lingering resentments a massacre would produce. Circumstances compelled Saladin to kill fellow Muslims; the faster the wounds healed the better.

Two important challenges had been faced down, but other more subtle dangers awaited Saladin. Mosul's young ruler al-Salih had many supporters who wanted Saladin dead. The preferred tool for such jobs in Saladin's day were killers known as Assassins. Led by an unscrupulous man named Rashid al-Din Sinan, the Assassins were a group of Shiite radicals opposed to the rule of the Sunni sultans or anyone even remotely resembling one. They controlled sizable chunks of territory both along the eastern Mediterranean coast and further inland. The suppression of this group stood near the top of Saladin's list of security measures, so the Assassins welcomed any overture suggesting that the sultan be eliminated, such as the one that secretly emanated from Aleppo.

Sinan, however, wanted to take the measure of this young Kurd-turned-sultan. If he could get Saladin to abandon his proposed campaign against the Assassins without bloodshed, so much the better. Sinan sent a messenger to Saladin who asked to speak privately with him. Being no fool, Saladin agreed to dismiss his entire guard, save two trusted mamluks whose loyalty was beyond question. Saladin felt safe putting his life in their hands. During the ensuing discussion, Sinan's man turned to the mamluks and calmly asked them, "If I ordered you . . . to kill this Sultan, would you do so?" The men promptly replied, "Command as you wish." A shocked Saladin got the point. He assured the messenger that he would ease the pressure on Sinan and his followers. If they could place their killers so close to him, the Assassins needed to be handled with more caution. Yet Saladin absorbed an even greater lesson that day. He realized that domestic matters required attention as close as that he gave to the Franks. Saladin understood that, from this point on, his power at home could never be taken for granted. Yet despite all the rebels, assassins, and other challenges faced by Saladin, he felt secure enough to turn to his real enemy—the Christians.

WAR AGAINST THE FRANKS: THE ROAD TO HATTIN

At age 45, Saladin ruled a vast area that stretched from Egypt in the west to the Euphrates River in the east, northward to modern-day Turkey, and southward to the Persian Gulf. His new domain encompassed the largest and wealthiest cities in Islam. The most lucrative trade centers, the best harbors, and the most fertile farmland fell under Saladin's control. Taken together, Saladin administered affairs for the greatest share of the world's Muslim population at the time, thus putting him in control of the heart of Islam.

Yet this responsibility obliged him to confront the dreaded Franks. Devotion to the care of Islam meant that Saladin necessarily committed himself to war against the crusader states—and hatred of the Christians now had to be transformed from raw emotion into action. In this developing drama, the Franks played their part as antagonists wonderfully. Never content with their substantial foothold in the Holy Land, the Europeans constantly harassed and encroached upon their Muslim neighbors, attacking a village here, a caravan there, and stinging like so many armored wasps. The crusaders buzzed for years along Islam's western border, and most Muslims had long since resigned themselves to the Christian presence. But Saladin was an exception. He never felt satisfied with sharing Palestine. He, in fact, looked forward to a war that would settle matters once and for all. With his power base secure, the moment seemed right for such a contest, and it was just at this moment that the Franks foolishly chose to provoke Saladin.

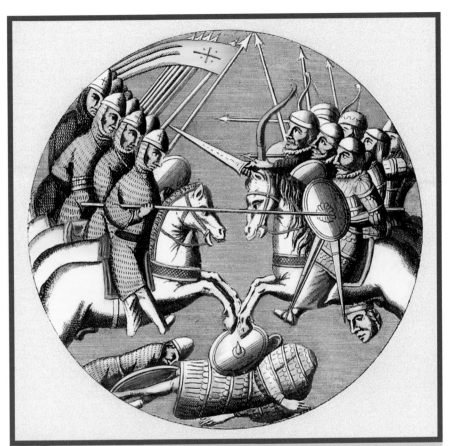

A painting depicting a battle between the Christian crusaders and Muslims. Once Saladin had quieted the rumblings within his own religion, he could assemble an army to combat the crusaders.

One crusader in particular, Reginald of Châtillon, took great pleasure in antagonizing the new sultan. Brutal and ambitious, Reginald had a reputation as a troublemaker even among his own people. He liked to stir things up and rarely did anything for anyone other than himself. Worse still, Reginald spoiled for a fight with Saladin—who, for his part, found intolerable the fact that this impulsive and impetuous Frank had taken up residence in the castle at Kerak. Virtually impregnable, Kerak loomed high above the crucial supply routes that linked Syria to Egypt. From his perch at Kerak, Reginald could swoop down on Muslim caravans at will, seizing their valuable cargo while, at the same time, mocking Saladin's ability to defend his realm.

Far from satisfied with the damage done by his raids out of Kerak, Reginald sought out every opportunity to humiliate and provoke the Muslims. One such effort culminated in an audacious raid on the Arabian city of Medina. Reginald planned a lightning attack on the city for the sole purpose of stealing the body of the long-dead prophet Muhammad. He then hoped to desecrate the body as an insult to all Islam. Unfortunately for the lord of Kerak, his ill-conceived escapade failed miserably. When news of the attempted raid reached Saladin, the sultan lashed out in a blind rage. Although Reginald slipped through Saladin's fingers, his Frankish accomplices did not, and the sultan vented his anger on them. By nature a more thoughtful and restrained man, Saladin could not suffer such a vile assault on the religion that gave substance to his very existence. Saladin ordered that the captured Franks, 170 in all, be paraded through the streets of Alexandria, Mecca, Medina, and Cairo, seated backwards on camels. After much humiliation, Saladin's instructions directed that the men pay the final price for their blasphemy: beheading.

So uncharacteristic was such retribution that his commanders did not follow through on Saladin's order at first. The sultan's own brother, Saif al-Din al-Adil, questioned his decision, prompting Saladin to write him an explanatory letter. The men must die, Saladin wrote, for two reasons, one practical and one personal. First, the raiders had almost made it all the way into one of the holiest cities in Islam undetected. If he let them live, they would certainly return by the same route with a larger, more determined force: "the enemy would flood into the sacred country," Saladin argued. Second, the honor of Islam cried out for revenge, for blood. The sultan contended that the Christian attack "was an unparalleled enormity in the history of Islam," and flatly declared, "Let the decision to kill them be carried out." The Koran prescribed and Saladin agreed that if infidels chose to fight Muslims "by the Holy Mosque . . . then slay them. Such is the requital for unbelievers" (Koran, 2:191). Although a man of virtually limitless compassion and thought, Saladin could not let infidels mock Islam and escape unscathed. He had pledged himself as a boy to the service and defense of Allah. As his very name made clear, Saladin understood Islam's well-being to be his unique responsibility, and he took it seriously. He could not let pass a flagrant assault on the Prophet and his faith.

After the executions of the Franks, Saladin turned to Reginald with a vengeance. In 1183, Saladin laid siege to Kerak. His attempt to punish Reginald, for all its ferocity, came to nothing as Kerak held fast. Meanwhile, matters in Christian Palestine took a turn for the worse. The young king of Jerusalem, Baldwin V, died suddenly in 1186 without a clear successor, and confusion instantly set in. The premier crusader state stood leaderless as grasping nobles descended on Jerusalem and scrambled to fill the void left by Baldwin's death.

Chief among the contenders for the throne were two very influential men, Guy of Lusignan and Raymond of Tripoli. Guy craftily outmaneuvered Raymond and took possession of Jerusalem by marrying Baldwin's mother. Needless to say, Raymond felt cheated. He had served as Baldwin's regent, acting virtually as king in the boy's stead, and he felt that the throne rightfully should have gone to him upon the king's death. Angry and humiliated, Raymond retreated to his castle at Tiberias near the Sea of Galilee and sulked.

Guy felt nothing but contempt for Islam, so Saladin correctly read hints of war in has accession. Unwilling to be caught by surprise, Saladin began preparing for a preemptive strike against the Christians. Reginald, knowing that Saladin might move while the struggle for power in Jerusalem distracted the Franks and aching for war with the Muslims, struck first. In early 1187, Reginald fell upon a massive caravan headed for Damascus from Egypt. The rogue crusader easily captured the juicy prize of trade goods carried by the camels and, even more valuable, found Saladin's sister among the travelers. The sultan's sister and the others with her demanded to be released, but Reginald, true to form, only laughed at their request. Openly, he mocked them saying, "Let your Muhammad come and deliver you." When word of the seizure and Reginald's haughty contempt reached Saladin's ears, he erupted in a fury. Saladin vowed to kill Reginald with his own hands and he spat out an order for jihad.

Saladin welcomed the opportunity to fulfill what he saw as his destiny. War with the Christians, he thought, was all part of God's plan; Allah wanted him, not Guy and Reginald, to have the Holy Land. As Saladin once remarked to his secretary, "When God gave me the land of Egypt, I'm sure he meant Palestine for me as well." Now the time had come to claim his gift.

Saladin began his campaign against the Franks by turning for help to an old acquaintance who ironically was a prominent Frank—Guy's rival Raymond of Tripoli. Unlike Guy, Raymond had lived his whole life in Palestine. He spoke fluent Arabic, and greatly admired the tenets and practice of Islam. He also had an immense respect for Saladin—even more so now that it appeared that Saladin might attack Guy. Raymond and Saladin had been at peace since they signed a truce in 1184, and the two leaders got along very well. Raymond on one occasion even sought Saladin's assistance during an earlier dispute with other Franks.

Saladin felt confident, considering the recent tussle in Jerusalem, that the lord of Tiberias might aid him in his effort to bring down Guy and, through him, Reginald. With Raymond's help, Saladin could avenge an insult against his family while opening the gates of Palestine to reconquest. So, Saladin asked Raymond for free passage through his lands. Fearing Saladin far less than the deceitful Guy, Raymond said yes, but he put conditions on his agreement: Saladin had only one day to pass; he could move only during daylight hours; and he had to foreswear any raiding of Frankish villages along the way. Saladin readily accepted Raymond's terms. Saladin's army, led by his son al-Afdal, marched out of Damascus bound for Palestine.

Raymond's followers immediately assailed him as a traitor to his people and Christ. The Hospitallers and Templars, orders of fighting monks who served under Raymond, rebelled. They had spent their lifetimes defending Christianity against the Muslims and now they were forced to sit by idly while a Muslim army passed unmolested under their very noses. They could not tolerate such an affront. Without permission, the Hospitallers and Templars attacked Saladin's column two miles north of Nazareth at a place called Cresson. Though undeniably courageous, the 400-man contingent of knights and foot soldiers stood little chance of turning back the Muslims and were destroyed in short order. The Muslim warriors enjoyed an easy victory and celebrated, in time-honored fashion, by cutting off the heads of their enemies and sticking them atop spears. Saladin received the good news from his own son in a letter that overflowed with joy. However, the Frankish defeat at Cresson had the unintended consequence of forcing Raymond off the fence he had been sitting on. He now had to choose between Saladin, with whom he felt a certain kinship, and his Christian brothers. Quietly, Raymond slipped out of Tiberias and announced his decision by going to Jerusalem and pledging his support for Guy.

Saladin felt deeply hurt by Raymond's defection. "He used us," the sultan raged, "to set to rights his own affairs and to terrify his fellow Franks." Now, Raymond had broken a solemn agreement and offered himself as a tool for Guy's use. Saladin,

A Knight Templar. The fighting monks of the Knights Templar and Hospitaller could not stand idly by and watch the Muslim army pass through their territory, even though it had been agreed upon through a truce between their leader Raymond of Tripoli and Saladin. The Templars and Hospitallers attempted to attack the Muslim army, but were quickly defeated.

fuming, immediately marched on Raymond's castle, bringing with him an army of around 24,000 fighting men. The sultan wanted, of course, to punish Raymond, but he also hoped that his move would prod Guy into action prematurely. He planned to draw the Franks into a decisive battle on ground of his choosing, where he could hand the Christians a crushing defeat that might open Palestine to the armies of Islam. Victory over the infidels became a real possibility.

The siege of Tiberias proceeded well enough, and Saladin exuded confidence. God did indeed seem to be on his side; even the stars seemed favorable. During the years 1186–1187, six solar and two lunar eclipses occurred, prompting the superstitious Franks to doubt their cause. King Guy's own chamberlain had a nightmare in which God used Saladin to punish the sinful Christians for failing to protect the Holy Land. Regardless of such ominous predictions, the real issue remained how Raymond and Guy would react to Saladin's thrust into Palestine. As the two Frankish leaders fretted and argued, Tiberias—save for the heavily fortified main citadel—surrendered. Firmly in control of matters now, Saladin sat back and, like a wily chess master, waited for the Christians' next move.

VICTORY AND BEYOND

THE HORNS OF HATTIN, JULY 4, 1187

News that a Frankish army had left Jerusalem reached Saladin just as he finished his prayers outside of Raymond's fortress at Tiberias early on a summer morning in 1187. Instantly he set out, hoping to intercept the advancing army at a point that suited him and favored Muslim tactics. Saladin found just the right place for a fight a few miles south of Tiberias on the lonely, desolate plain of Lubiya. Table-flat and wide open, the plain gave the advantage to a mobile force such as that composed of horse archers, which he possessed. The area was also bone-dry. Saladin's withered opponents would have no water to slake their thirst as they moved forward. Lubiya offered a bleak setting for the coming battle, its featureless vistas broken only by the village of Hattin and a low set of hills known as the Horns.

Guy responded to Saladin's move into Palestine with characteristic

The Horns of Hattin marked a major victory for Saladin over the crusader army led by Guy of Lusignan. Afterwards, Saladin had 230 of the Knights Templar and Hospitaller beheaded, while the rest of the army was sold into slavery. Additionally, he had his nemesis Reginald beheaded.

impulsiveness and reckless abandon. In his haste to engage the Muslims, Guy selected a line of march that took him and his army directly across the blistering sand and gravel of Lubiya. Even though the crusader king knew that his men would bake in their suffocating suits of heavy chain mail, he deliberately led them into a place wholly unsuited to European battle tactics and miles from the nearest source of plentiful freshwater, the

Sea of Galilee. Worse yet, because Guy's march could be so easily tracked by Muslim scouts, blocking his way and perhaps even surrounding his force would not prove difficult. Saladin's cavalry screen not only harassed Guy from the moment he stepped onto the plain but kept the sultan updated on every Frankish move. As the searing July day wore on, the odds and the elements turned against the crusaders. Saladin, in fact, thought Guy's course of action to be so foolish that perhaps "Satan incited Guy to do what ran counter to his purpose."

Guy's route not only gave the advantage to Saladin, but his marching order could not have been crafted better by Saladin himself. The crusaders formed up in the traditional fashion with the precious heavy cavalry—the armored shock troops that represented the core of any medieval European army—inside a wall-like protective cordon of infantry, the rearguard of which marched backwards when confronted by an enemy. The Franks struck an impressive pose, but they were slow and clumsy in the march. Their burden of chain mail, huge swords, helmets, and lances bore down on them and provided metal surfaces that acted like oven walls in the hot sun. The crusaders suffered terribly from the heat and even more from the gradually intensifying attacks by the swift, mobile Muslim horse archers. Arrows, fired by the fleet horsemen, tortured the plodding Franks, who had no choice but to trudge onward.

Saladin recognized the flaws in Guy's strategy and maneuvered his army between the crusaders and the life-giving water that the Franks needed so desperately. Next, he swung the wings of his army to either side of Guy's column so as to guide the crusaders, in a sense, onto ground that favored mounted assaults. Swarms of Muslim infantrymen backed up the horse archers both to protect Saladin's baggage and supplies and also to lend a fixed point from which any attack could begin and end. Armed with spears and bows, these men would be used to finish off the crusaders Saladin hoped to surround and destroy. As the sultan positioned his army, his commanders unfurled multicolored banners that slowly began to flutter in the warm breeze, the sound of drums called *naqqara* echoed off the Horns, trumpets blared, and cymbals clanged announcing the Muslims' presence to the Franks. Pestered by archers and worn down by the sun, Guy responded by reluctantly calling a halt to the march and ordering his men to set up camp.

As the brilliant July sun peeked over the horizon that following morning, Guy must have known this would be a very long day for him and his men. The king renewed the march, hoping to beat the sun in his race to find water and engage his Muslim enemy. Saladin's cavalry screen detected the Frankish movement as Guy's army rolled slowly forward, and the flank attacks began. Horse archers darted in and out of range, showering arrows on the Franks in assaults that increased in both frequency and ferocity as the day wore on. Saladin, sensing an opportunity to innovate, ordered the scrub brush along Guy's axis of advance set ablaze. The resulting fires simultaneously elevated the ambient temperature that nature had already driven to unbearable heights while producing a thick cloud of acrid smoke that obscured the Franks' vision and stung their eyes.

Confusion quickly set in. The knights could not see! Their horses reared and spun. Arrows seemed to come from nowhere and everywhere. The crusaders' anxieties rose with the heat from the fires surrounding them. In stark terror, the men bunched up and suddenly panicked. Their ranks broke and soldiers began to scatter in all directions, and each one ran for his life. Saladin chose this instant to strike. His lancers and archers pounced down on the hapless Franks. Some men screamed as lances pierced their chain mail; others writhed on the ground like human pincushions shot through with arrow shafts. Though the odds and the ground stood against them, some tenacious knights fought valiantly. Slashing at their attackers, the armored men kept enough of their noble composure to try, unsuccessfully, to rally the foot soldiers who ran here and there seeking safety from the onrushing Muslims. The knights, invoking the age-old cry of death with honor, launched one suicidal charge after another. Frantically, they tried to claw their way out of the trap Saladin had sprung. But the last futile charges failed, and Guy was forced to surrender.

As soon as the dust had settled, Saladin commanded that the proud Knights Hospitaller and Templar be given their just desserts for offending Islam over the years in their words and deeds. The sultan had 230 of them beheaded. Saladin ordered the rest of the survivors rounded up. The victors placed collars around their necks and chains on their wrists, and led them away to be sold as slaves in the markets of Damascus. So many captives flooded into Saladin's capital that the price of slaves plummeted. Standing on the auction block, humiliated, most Franks could not even bring a decent price. One Muslim reportedly bought a crusader for a pair of old sandals.

A dismal fate awaited the common soldier captured at Hattin, but worse befell Guy and Saladin's archenemy, Reginald. Soon after the fighting and beheading stopped, Saladin had his two defeated adversaries brought before him. Guy, visibly nervous, asked the sultan about his fate. Saladin responded by handing him a cup of sherbet sweetened with rose water. Muslim tradition held that once the victor had given refreshment to the vanquished, the latter's life was safe. Guy tried to pass the cup to Reginald, but Saladin blocked his hand. The sultan demanded an apology from Reginald for his depredations and offered him conversion to Islam. Reginald, true to form, sarcastically replied that he had nothing to apologize for: "Kings have always acted thus," explained the lord of Kerak. "I did nothing more." Saladin paused for a moment and then flew into a rage. "Pig!" he shouted. "You are my prisoner and yet you answer me so arrogantly!" A guard hustled the Frankish leaders out of Saladin's presence only to have Reginald swiftly recalled. Next, Saladin sent for Guy. As the king of Jerusalem walked in, a slave dragged Reginald's headless body past him.

The city of Tyre, led by Conrad of Montferrat, was bypassed by Saladin when it was obvious that it would take a long and bloody siege to take it. Even Saladin's threat to kill the commander's own father did not sway Conrad—in fact, he himself shot an arrow at his own father.

Saladin had fulfilled his promise and had even used his own curved sword to take Reginald's life.

Trembling on his knees and probably uttering a thousand prayers in his head, Guy stared at Saladin. Suddenly, the sultan spoke in a soothing voice. "Real kings do not kill each other," Saladin reassured his captive. "He was no king, and he overstepped his limits." Before being sent off to prison, Guy felt Saladin's grace once again; the sultan offered him another bowl of cool sherbet.

JERUSALEM

Saladin moved quickly to follow up on his stunning victory. Splitting his forces, he marched on the most important and dangerous Christian strong point in all Palestine, Tyre. Tyre possessed a large garrison and was protected by gigantic, well-constructed walls. The city's commander, moreover, was one of the ablest of the Frankish leaders, Conrad of Montferrat. Conrad respected Saladin but did not fear him, and he was determined to deny the sultan control of Tyre. Saladin knew that a direct assault on the city would fail and that a prolonged siege would be difficult and counterproductive, so he tried a bit of persuasion, only to find Conrad unimpressed. Saladin had Conrad's father, who had been captured at Hattin, brought to the city walls in chains; there he threatened to kill the elderly man if Conrad did not yield. The Frank's reply shocked and disappointed Saladin. "Tie him to the stake. What do I care?" shouted Conrad from the walls. "I shall be the first to shoot him. For he is old and worthless." Conrad then picked up a crossbow and launched a bolt at his own father. Saladin shook his head and pronounced Conrad to be despicable and "very cruel," but he got the message; Tyre would fall only after much bloodshed and time. Time was one thing the sultan did not have. Saladin gathered his army together and moved on, leaving Tyre in Christian hands.

Saladin's fortunes improved a bit after Tyre. One by one the other cities fell—Caesarea, Jaffa, Arsuf. Finally, Saladin stood before Ascalon. An ancient city, Ascalon was the gateway to Egypt. Its possession would provide a secure trade and communications link between Egypt and Syria, the two halves of Saladin's realm. The sultan needed Ascalon badly and quickly if he wanted to maintain the momentum of his campaign. The city, however, held out. Ascalon rejected all of Saladin's demands for surrender. Even hauling the unfortunate Guy out of prison and having him ask for the city gates to be opened did no good. Ascalon's defenders merely laughed at Guy's pleading, notwithstanding the fact that their surrender would purchase his freedom. Faced with such defiance, Saladin reluctantly ordered his engineers to begin undermining Ascalon's walls. Digging replaced dealing, but the memory of Alexandria haunted the sultan. Though on the outside this time, Saladin still detested sieges and the privation they brought. Luckily for him, Ascalon's leaders found the prospect of bombardment, starvation, and massacre equally unappealing. Soon after the work began on bringing down the city's walls, the elders opened their gates and came out begging for mercy. The gateway to Egypt surrendered.

One siege had been averted, but another greater one loomed ahead. Jerusalem's defenders would surely resist more vigorously than their compatriots at Ascalon. Ascalon's value lay only in its geographic location, but Jerusalem was the Holy City, the city of Christ. To give it up without a fight would be to give up the heart of Christianity. Saladin recognized the significance of Jerusalem to the Christians, so he chose to offer the people of the city very liberal terms of surrender before marching on it. The sultan cordially received an embassy from Jerusalem while camped outside Ascalon and demonstrated his legendary generosity. Saladin promised a siege but not a serious one. The Muslim army would take up positions around Jerusalem, according to the plan he outlined, but daily life within its walls could proceed unmolested. Farmers supplying the city with food could continue to till their fields and feed Jerusalem's population without fear. In return, the city had to agree to surrender without armed resistance if no Frankish army came to its rescue by the following spring. Saladin furthermore assured them that the citizens of Jerusalem would not be harmed.

Much to his surprise and chagrin, the men rejected all of Saladin's terms out of hand. Rather than give Jerusalem to the Muslims, the ambassadors swore that they and their colleagues would "die in defense of the Lord's sepulcher, for how could we do otherwise?" The response left Saladin no choice; Jerusalem would be stormed.

The Holy City lay only a day's march from Ascalon. Saladin's army covered the distance quickly and easily. Soon, the Muslims stood before the city's walls, and prepared to launch their assault. Inside Jerusalem, 6,000 fighting men led by Balian of Ibelin waited in defense. The following siege was short but bloody and ended only when Saladin shifted position to that taken by the crusaders in 1099, brought down the walls, charged in, and forced the gallant Balian to capitulate.

The Muslims had been compelled to take Jerusalem by force; they now had the right by tradition to rampage through its streets. Saladin, however, had already decided to deny his men their customary orgy of destruction. For one thing, he did not want to harden Christian resolve in the future or give them an emotional cause to fight for as the slaughter of 1099 had done with the Muslims. A peaceful occupation would create no martyrs to be avenged. But Saladin's personality argued against wanton killing as well. Saladin killed for Islam and Islam's god, but he never enjoyed it. While at war, Saladin often found comfort in the Koran, and perhaps none of its verses expressed his emotions better than the one that read, "Enjoined on you is fighting, and this you abhor" (Koran, 2:216). Saladin found nothing but heartache in war, and certainly wanted nothing to do with murdering innocent people, even if they were nonbelievers.

Still, he had taken Jerusalem by force; the sultan could only show so much mercy without undercutting his authority and image in his men's eyes. His emirs and his soldiers clamored for revenge. Tradition demanded some kind of punishment for the Christians and reward for the Muslims. Thinking hard and fast, Saladin arrived at a compromise that would satisfy his army and his own conscience. He set a ransom, on a sliding scale, for the entire population: those worth more in terms of social class and prominence would pay more, those worth less would pay

Upon entering Jerusalem in 1187, Saladin did not destroy any places of worship, including those of the Christians. He also restored the Dome of the Rock (shown here) and the al-Aqsa mosque, two very sacred places to Muslims.

less. Yet regardless of social status, all the inhabitants able to raise their ransom would be free to leave. Everyone else would be locked in chains and led away as slaves. Saladin figured that once the lust for revenge and thirst for gain had been sated, he could get down to the real business of returning Jerusalem to Islam. The sultan planned to restore the city's holy places, improve its public works, and repair its fortifications. The new Jerusalem would be a gift to God.

As the evacuation process got underway, Saladin entered

the city in triumph. On October 2, 1187, Saladin rode into Jerusalem. Immediately his heart sank. The Christian religious and political elite exploited his generosity by hoarding Jerusalem's wealth while making no provision for the ransom of their poverty-stricken neighbors. The Church especially enriched itself while the poor suffered. Saladin's captains urged him to violate his own terms and step in to put an end to the flagrant abuse. The sight of religious leaders abandoning their flock troubled Saladin and offended his sense of honor. He took pity on the widows and children of fallen Christian knights, releasing them of his own accord without ransom, and arranged for the freeing of a few other pitiable occupants of Jerusalem's poor neighborhoods. But the Koran ordered Muslims to "abide by your oaths" (Koran, 5:89), and the sultan was a man of his word. To his commanders, Saladin explained that he would obey the letter of the agreement he had reached with Balian "so that they are unable to accuse the Believers of breaking their word." When the last of those able to scrape together their ransom left Jerusalem, Saladin watched regretfully as his troops marched 8,000 poor souls off into bondage.

Saladin's tenure at Jerusalem spoke to his true qualities of thoughtfulness, compassion, and devotion to Islam. Against the wishes of his men, Saladin did not destroy the Church of the Holy Sepulcher or any other Christian place of worship. He warmly welcomed back the Jews whom the Christians had driven from Jerusalem and persecuted mercilessly throughout the territory held by the Franks. Saladin restored the Dome of the Rock, the place where it was said Muhammad once stepped up into heaven leaving behind his footprint in solid stone, and he refurbished the al-Aqsa mosque that celebrated that event to the delight of the Muslim faithful. Still, Saladin's benevolence hurt his cause. By not halting the flow of wealth out of Jerusalem during the evacuation, Saladin lost untold sums of money he would need later on. His release of Balian set a dangerous opponent free to cause trouble down the road. Future victories would be harder because of Saladin's reluctance to compromise his honesty and honor.

Other bad omens hung over Saladin's great triumph at Jerusalem. While the sultan restored the Holy City, the fortress at Tyre grew stronger by the day as refugees and supplies flowed in. Tyre, in fact, slowly became impregnable and began to emerge as a focal point of crusader resistance and counterattack. Like Tyre, other Christian cities battened down and prepared to defend themselves while Saladin tarried at Jerusalem. Saladin's future strategy, worse yet, now became transparent to everyone; his enemies could readily anticipate his next move. The chess master unexpectedly found himself playing on the defensive. Saladin had won Jerusalem but lost the initiative. The physical manifestation of this change stood along the Palestinian coast in the form of one massive walled city—Acre.

THE SIEGE
OF ACRE

Jerusalem belonged to Saladin. The sultan now had to settle on
what to do next. Looking over the strategic situation, Saladin
decided to strike northward in order to protect his vulnerable flank
against a European invasion through Byzantine territory. He also
wanted to eliminate as many potential staging areas for a counterattack
against Jerusalem as possible by hitting places like Antioch and
perhaps Tyre once again. If he could dominate the coast, Saladin
would also effectively choke off supplies and the flow of reinforcements to the inland castles.

Quickly, he put his plan into action. The primary northern
strong point of Antioch fell on September 16, and thus a dangerous
invasion route had been blocked. Secure in the north, the sultan
turned southward toward Tyre, which stuck like a bone in the
Muslim throat. The city's sizable, well-supplied garrison sat behind
25-foot-thick walls and mocked Saladin by its continued resistance.

Antioch in Syria was quickly conquered by Saladin while en route to staging counterattacks by the crusaders. The Christian crusaders would be trying to get Jerusalem back, and Saladin had to defend it while attempting to expand his region of control.

The sultan gave some thought to besieging Tyre, but chose once again to bypass it as he had after Hattin. Farther inland, he likewise avoided dealing with the powerful castle known as Krak des Chevaliers. Reginald's old fortress at Kerak, however, proved to be a less formidable challenge. Saladin took it, and with its capture picked up a needed psychological boost while removing a very real threat to the interior trade routes from Egypt and Arabia.

Confident in his good fortune, Saladin let his generosity get the better of him. He made a fatal error in judgment that would cost him dearly in the near future. In July 1188, he released Guy of Lusignan from prison. Guy, as a condition of his release, swore on oath that he would not fight Saladin again. Once free, though, Guy retreated to Tripoli and swiftly broke his word. Informed by a priest that a promise made to a Muslim was not binding, Guy renounced his oath, raised an army against Saladin, and, after a brief confrontation with Conrad at Tyre, prepared to attack the Muslims. Guy chose the city of Acre as his target.

THE SIEGE, 1189–1191

Guy appeared outside of Acre's walls in August 1189 and laid siege to the city. In a single stroke, the Muslim garrison found itself boxed in with its back to the Mediterranean Sea. Saladin immediately marched in relief and took up positions around the Christian line. The besiegers were now themselves besieged. In concentric half-circles, the Muslims and Christians faced each other, with the Franks sandwiched between opponents on either side. Fierce battles raged as the Franks tried to break into Acre while Saladin worked to smash through the Christian lines and rescue the trapped garrison. Neither army saw much success. Acre's resolute defenders held out; Guy's force showed not the slightest sign of budging; Saladin's grip on the Franks never loosened—a stalemate.

Stress once again overcame Saladin, and he fell ill. Weak and feverish, Saladin received unwelcome news that a large European army was headed his way. The German king, Frederick Barbarossa, was on the move with an army reported to number 250,000 fighting men. (Actually, Barbarossa commanded only about 50,000.) Such a force could easily smash through Saladin's siege lines and annihilate Acre's garrison. The sultan, on his sickbed, slipped into depression as he imagined what would happen when Frederick's army arrived. Saladin needed a miracle, and, as had happened so many times in the past, he got one. During a river crossing in Cilicia, a region in what is today southern Turkey, Frederick decided to shun a low bridge in favor of crossing the river on horseback. His mount lost its footing and threw the king into the water, where he drowned. Without Barbarossa's inspiration and leadership, the German army dissolved. Only about 5,000 men made it to Acre—not nearly enough to make a difference in the course of the battle.

Saladin, encouraged by the evaporation of the German threat, recovered and was fit for duty by mid-January 1190. But bad news once again reached the sultan's ears. The capture of Jerusalem had caused an outcry among the Christians of France and England. A new Crusade had been declared. The call went out for fighting men, and money was raised through a special tax aptly named the Saladin Tithe. French knights, led by their king, Philip II, were slinging swords, strapping on armor, and preparing to embark for Palestine. English soldiers did likewise, led by their monarch, Richard I, also known as Lionheart.

Lionheart was a dangerous opponent. Richard was a proven and capable warrior who had cut his teeth on a series of wars against his own father. Although he would technically be second in command to Philip, Richard was the real leader of the invasion force that Saladin would soon have to deal with. The crusader army itself was bound for Tyre, then to Acre, where it would link up with Guy. Once joined, the two forces planned to hold off the relief army while strangling the Muslim garrison. The tide was rapidly turning against Saladin.

Philip went to the Holy Land first, while Richard left their staging area in Sicily for Cyprus. He took his time conquering the island, seeming to be in no hurry to move on to the real show further east. Meanwhile, Saladin watched as the crusader ring tightened around Acre; the arrival of Philip's army did not help. Within Acre's walls, the Muslims suffered miserably, a fact communicated to Saladin by carrier pigeons and swimmers

Philip II of France led soldiers from his country on a new crusade against Saladin. Joining Philip II was Richard I from England. In fact, there was a tithe called the Saladin Tithe that was employed to collect money for this particular campaign.

who slipped quietly through the lines by entering the city from the sea—the only forms of communication that could still get through.

Worse yet, Guy had constructed tall siege towers over the months complemented by battering rams and giant claws known as "cats." While the machines went to work, Saladin sat there, frustrated and helpless. The most important contribution to Acre's continued survival at this crucial point, in fact, came not from Saladin but from a lowly Syrian engineer. Faced with the problem of destroying the huge siege towers that threatened to topple Acre's walls, the engineer developed a form of "Greek fire," a flammable liquid derived from naphtha that not only burned hotly but also exploded on impact. Using this invention, the Muslims destroyed two Frankish towers and saved the city, at least for the time being. Saladin watched as a mere spectator during this episode, a fact that revealed the changing fortunes of war and fame.

Dissent among Saladin's emirs grew as the siege dragged on. Commanders began to grumble, and then to leave. Here and there small groups of fighters drifted away from the frontlines, led by men who had become disillusioned with the jihad and Saladin. The sultan, showing the strain, snapped at one departing commander that he could expect no help from Saladin in the future. "At one time you asked for my protection," Saladin roared. "Now look out for another protector." Notwithstanding Saladin's angry recriminations, emirs continued to pull out, and those that stayed questioned Saladin's leadership and judgment as never before.

By the end of 1190, the siege of Acre left Saladin a changed man. Now 52 years old, Saladin fought in vain against the contradictions and internal conflicts that had plagued him since his youth. Always torn between his father, the politician, and his uncle, the fighter, between political necessity and religious devotion, between violence and peace, Saladin stood before Acre virtually paralyzed by indecision and doubt. He became, as a result, a prisoner of events as they unfolded. Saladin never wanted war and now sought to soften its sharp edge. Although victory required unforgiving toughness, Saladin gave play to his compassionate side as he tried to reconcile the disparate elements of his personality. Once during the heat of battle, for example, a Frankish woman came to Saladin begging him to spare the life of her three-month-old baby, kidnapped by Muslim raiders the night before. Ashamed of his troops' conduct in taking the child, Saladin personally returned the infant to its mother and gave them safe passage back to the crusader lines. Saladin likewise freed an elderly Frank captured at Acre. The sultan was touched by the man's simple, heartfelt piety. Another time, Saladin stopped his own sons from killing a group of prisoners. He chastised them, saying he did not want them to "become accustomed in their youth to the shedding of blood and laugh at it." Indeed, Saladin probably would have broken off the siege altogether if he had not convinced himself that "abandonment [of the jihad] is a sin. . . . "

Saladin grew more conflicted as he grew older, and felt it more than ever as he sat outside the Christian lines at Acre. As each day passed, the sultan fought more with himself and less with his Christian foes. When Saladin surveyed the landscape around him, his worst fears rose prominently before his eyes: powerful enemies everywhere, trusted friends nowhere, and a Muslim city slowly being strangled with the great Sultan of Egypt and Syria unable to do a thing about it.

THE FALL OF ACRE

On April 20, 1191, with the siege in full swing and Acre still bottled up, Philip of France arrived with his army of fresh crusaders. Philip brought a sense of renewal with him and a redoubled determination to capture Acre. The battering of the city's defenses became much more intense. Mangonels such as the one nicknamed the "Evil Neighbor" hurled huge rocks at Acre's towers and pounded the battlements, "cats" scratched at the walls, and battering rams hammered away at the massive stone ramparts. Meanwhile, engineers dug incessantly under the walls hoping to reduce them to a pile of rubble. Every day the garrison grew weaker and the defense more hopeless under the fury of the Frankish assault.

The sun that rose on June 7 heralded the darkest day for Saladin. That morning, Richard of England announced the

In 1191, the siege of Acre ended with the crusaders taking the city and the Muslims inside surrendering—but also opening surrender negotiations against Saladin's orders, giving the victors far more spoils than Saladin would have allowed.

arrival of his fleet and army by sinking a critical supply ship carrying food and around 700 crack troops bound for Saladin. With Richard's appearance aboard his personal war galley, *Trenchemere*, the entire character of the siege changed. Richard had no intention of letting Philip get the credit when Acre fell, so he immediately began taking control of operations. He ratcheted up the pace and the fierceness of the bombardment, while oddly enough trying to open peace talks with Saladin himself. Ever gracious, Saladin responded to Richard's overtures by sending the English king gifts of fruit and snow; Lionheart, not to be outdone, gave Saladin a personal slave. Saladin, however, for all his gallantry, refused a meeting with Richard, saying, "It is not customary for kings to meet. . . . For, after they have spoken together and given one another tokens of mutual confidence, it is not seemly for them to return to making war upon one another." The siege went on.

Richard tightened the noose around Acre. The walls of the city trembled as he battered them relentlessly. The king's men burrowed furiously below Acre's defenses, while Muslim engineers dug their own counter-tunnels, and strange subterranean battles broke out whenever the two contingents of miners met in the eerie darkness. Still, Acre held out. Richard at one point became so frustrated by the resilience of Acre's defenders that he even shouldered a crossbow himself and began shooting Muslim troops from the ramparts. As the fighting grew more intense, both sides could sense the climax coming.

Saladin, growing anxious, sought another meeting with Richard, but the Englishman rejected the offer of talks with the sultan. Desperate, Saladin took it upon himself to lead a brave but forlorn attack on the Christian lines. Mounting his horse and drawing his sword, Saladin cried out, "On for Islam!" The sultan, however, possessed more pluck than his men did. Some Muslim soldiers openly mutinied and refused to fight; other warriors fought half-heartedly. A few emirs flatly challenged Saladin's fitness for command; one went so far as to accuse the sultan of being responsible for the jihad's imminent failure before Acre. "You will destroy all Islam!" barked the emir. Saladin, dejected, broke off the assault and retreated to his tent to await the certain surrender of the garrison inside Acre.

Acre fell on July 12, 1191. Saladin reportedly cried at the sight of Christian war banners fluttering above the city. Disobeying Saladin's strict orders, the city's defenders had opened negotiations with Richard. Adding to the insult, they had done so in Saladin's name. The sultan, for his part, only learned of the proposed peace terms *after* they had been arranged. The Muslims, according to the cease-fire agreement, had to free 500 Christian prisoners, pay the Franks 200,000 gold pieces, and return a fragment of the True Cross of Christ the Muslims had seized at Hattin. Saladin had no choice; he initiated the process of meeting the victors' demands. Saladin responded slowly, however, so slowly that Richard began to suspect that the sultan was stalling, perhaps in anticipation of reinforcements from Egypt. As the days passed, news arrived from England that Richard's brother, John, was positioning himself to take the throne from the king. Every moment wasted waiting for the dilatory Saladin put Richard's continued monarchy in more doubt. Richard became increasingly nervous and, finally, he lost his patience. In a blind rage, Richard had 3,000 Muslim prisoners dragged outside Acre's gates. There, in full view of Saladin's horrified army, he had the men beheaded.

Saladin's response, while understandable, was totally out of character and reflected the strain and the frustrations of a lifetime spent combating a resourceful and tenacious foe. Saladin proclaimed his intention to someday sail to England "and pursue [the Christians] until no one remains on the face of the earth. . . . " More immediately, Saladin ordered that, henceforth, Christian captives were to be summarily executed. There would be no more mercy, no more compassion. Age, disappointment, and the brutality of war left Saladin bitter and broken. The end of his jihad was not far off.

SHOWDOWN AT THE HOLY CITY

RICHARD'S COASTAL MARCH

S aladin desperately sought battle with Richard after the disaster at Acre. He could sense his power declining and the confidence of the Muslim world slipping away. People began to doubt Saladin—and worse, he started to doubt himself. The sultan's moods swung wildly as he experienced alternating bouts of buoyant optimism and dark pessimism. Through it all, he sought solace in his beloved Koran. One of Saladin's favorite passages promised Allah's grace to those who never lost faith: "To those who fight strenuously in the cause of God . . . the Lord will be forgiving and merciful." Saladin eagerly anticipated the opportunity to fight strenuously for Islam; he wanted so badly to fight Richard that he could concentrate on nothing else. In time, Richard gave him such an opportunity.

By late August 1191, the crusaders were on the move. Richard broke camp around Acre and began a slow but steady march down

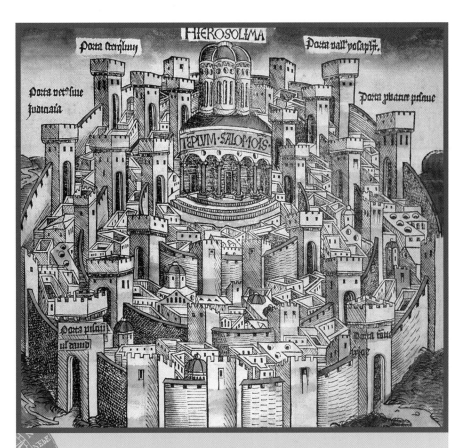

HIEROSOLIMA

TEPLVM·SALOMOIS

Eventually the armies of Saladin and Richard would end up facing each other at Jerusalem. While it was still under Muslim rule, the crusaders had won an impressive string of victories and were on their way to attempting to take the Holy City again.

the coast. His men, fully armed and accompanied by a long, heavily laden baggage train, followed a course along the beach that led them between the sea and the grassy coastal marshes and oak forests of Palestine. Richard selected his route so that he could maintain contact with the war galleys that protected his right flank and kept his army supplied. Although the sand and the marsh grass made the going tough, the crusaders adopted the standard marching formation. Like Guy's expedition at Hattin, Richard's men formed up with the heavy cavalry surrounded by a protective cordon of infantry. This plodding, boxlike mass of men and weapons inched down the coast like a slowly advancing dagger aimed at either Ascalon or Jerusalem. Saladin did not have a clue as to which critical stronghold served as the crusaders' objective.

Unsure about Richard's ultimate target, Saladin positioned his army for flank attacks rather than a head-on blocking move. The sultan hoped to harass and distract the Franks to the point where they would make some disastrous mistake. What Saladin envisaged was a battle like Hattin, where Christian miscalculations could be turned to his advantage. Saladin hoped for a decisive battle on his terms, on ground favorable to his tactics. The script seemed to have been already written: provoke an ill-advised halt in the Christian march, then pounce on the stationary prey. But Richard of England was no King Guy, and he refused to take Saladin's bait. Rather than stopping to fight the Muslims who pestered his flank and rearguard, the crusaders beat off their Muslim pursuers while on the move. Muslim arrows slowed but did not halt the crusader column.

Richard's men drove forward through sand and arrows battling enemies large and small. In addition to Muslim horsemen, the Franks had to contend with the snakes and scorpions that inhabited the beach. Some soldiers tried moving into the tall marsh grass in order to improve their pace only to meet up with huge tarantulas and even an occasional crocodile. Richard could not help his men contend with Palestine's wildlife, but his ingenuity did mitigate the effects of one natural element— the heat. The king kept his men fresh and relatively cool by alternating periods of marching and rest, the rest coming between Muslim attacks. He also kept the pace fairly steady if a bit brisk. Few men, however, were seriously tempted to fall out, no matter how hard it might have been to struggle onward. Muslim patrols were everywhere. Anyone who straggled behind or dropped out risked catching a well-placed arrow, or capture and the certainty of being sold into slavery.

Richard's determination to drive on regardless of Muslim pressure only increased Saladin's frustration and provoked his anger. Ever since Acre, Saladin's temper had grown worse and more unpredictable. Embittered by defeat, Saladin lost his reluctance to kill. His nature turned dark, and Christian prisoners now felt the sultan's full fury. Gone were the days of mercy and pity. Saladin, for the first time in his life, did not seek counsel in the Koran. Its verses prescribing the just and lenient treatment of prisoners went unheeded. Captives could expect no quarter, no matter who they were or how pitifully they pleaded for their lives. One Hungarian noble, captured when he foolishly but courageously charged alone into a group of Muslim archers, lost his head on Saladin's orders even though he begged on his knees for the sultan to spare him. On another occasion, Saladin had one miserable bunch of prisoners after another paraded before him to appeal forlornly to his merciful side. The sultan condemned each one and had them executed. Saladin even went so far as to have a female prisoner beheaded; she had been captured in full battle array. The vicious reality of war had taken its toll on the once kind and considerate Saladin.

ARSUF, SEPTEMBER 1191

Nothing Saladin could do had any effect on Richard's inexorable march toward what now appeared to be his most likely target, Ascalon. The English king pushed forward with single-minded determination through sand, field, and forest. He fought spirited flank and rearguard actions that succeeded in keeping the Muslims at bay. Richard's knights, however, grew weary of simply holding their course. The hit-and-run attacks by Saladin's horse archers tormented and enraged them. These armored warriors were proud, violent men and Richard's refusal to give battle appeared somewhat cowardly to them. They wanted to fight!

The soldiers reached the limits of their patience near the city of Arsuf on a sunny September day in 1191. During one of

Richard's march towards Ascalon was met with pressure from Saladin's army, but finally Richard's own army decided to stand and fight instead of merely marching on and defending themselves. At Arsuf, Saladin's army fell apart and ran for their lives, and Saladin suffered one of his most humiliating defeats.

the routine Muslim raids, a small group of knights took it upon themselves to strike back. The men had strict orders to ignore their antagonists and ride on, but enough was enough. As Muslim archers peppered the men with arrows from behind, the horsemen suddenly wheeled around and broke into a full charge. Richard's errant knights rode down furiously upon Saladin's surprised troops. The Christians, leveling their deadly lances from saddles mounted high on huge warhorses, thundered through the Muslim ranks. Men screamed in terror as the knights first punctured the line and then turned to hunt them down. Saladin's light cavalry was no match for such an awesome thrust; his soldiers ran. Despite his frantic efforts to rally them, panicked men streamed past Saladin paying no attention to his battlefield exhortations. The desperate Muslims sought safety, not martyrdom. When the fleeing army finally halted, Saladin looked back on 7,000 dead warriors. Arsuf had been a catastrophe. What should have been a minor action on the periphery of the Christian march turned into one of Saladin's worst defeats. For days afterward, Saladin refused to speak to anyone and took no food at all.

Eventually, Saladin shook himself out of his melancholy and gathered up the shattered remnants of his army. Rallying his commanders, the sultan began devising a new strategy to stop the seemingly unstoppable Richard. Yet Saladin's old nemesis, indecision, rose up to haunt him again. He had thought all along that Richard aimed to take either Jerusalem or Ascalon—but which one? Where should the Muslim defenses be concentrated? Should he make a stand at Ascalon, the portal to Egypt, or should he fall back on the Holy City, the traditional Christian prize, and fortify it strongly? Saladin dithered over these two options, perhaps hoping that Richard would make up his mind for him by moving definitively in one direction or the other. Saladin never seems to have considered the alternative avenues open to him. For one, he might have followed up the debacle at Arsuf with another attack on the Christians before they had time to collect themselves. Even a victorious army requires time to get back on its feet after battle. During this interval, a regrouping foe can be caught off guard if the assault is energetic and well led. Saladin could have distracted his opponent with a Nur al-Din–like strike far to Richard's rear. A cut across Richard's supply lines or a raid on Acre might have knocked the crusaders off balance and caused them to rethink their move down the coast. Another option would have been to maneuver somehow between Richard and the sea, hoping to detach him from his supply galleys. Unable to decide what to do next, Saladin settled on a very traditional but ultimately defensive course of action. The sultan chose, in the end, to deny Richard both Ascalon and Jerusalem. Saladin and his army began withdrawing toward Jerusalem, while orders went out to destroy Ascalon stone by stone. Richard would conquer a heap of rubble.

Nothing hurt Saladin more than feeling compelled to erase Ascalon. He told a friend that he took "God to witness I would rather lose all my children than cast a single stone from [Ascalon's] walls, but God wills it; it is necessary for the Muslim cause, therefore I am obliged to carry it through." Saladin could not defend two places at once, and Jerusalem was far more important to the jihad than Ascalon, so the latter would have to be sacrificed. Ascalon's destruction would prevent Richard's using the city as a crucial base of operations and force a battle at Jerusalem that might decide the war. The Third Crusade edged nearer to its climax.

Evacuating and dismantling Ascalon proved to be difficult. The walls and towers had to be baked by massive bonfires first to make them brittle, then engineers went to work on them with hammers. Slowly they smashed the walls to pieces and brought down the towers with a thunderous roar. Next, support facilities and houses were leveled. Families being evacuated turned back as they shuffled slowly away and watched as their homes collapsed in clouds of dust. The workers, once they finished, gathered up their equipment and marched hurriedly to rejoin Saladin. They left Ascalon uninhabitable; Richard's long, bloody excursion would gain him nothing. As the Muslim army retreated, it burned or wrecked anything that might be of use to the crusaders. This often meant laying waste to entire villages, setting fire to crops, and polluting wells. The Muslims supplemented these scorched-earth tactics with stinging raids

Saladin agonized over one of the hardest choices of his military career when he decided to dismantle the city of Ascalon in Palestine so that Richard would have nothing to conquer. Ascalon would be sacrificed so that Saladin could pool his resources into defending Jerusalem.

against Richard's flanks and vicious attacks on crusader patrols and foraging parties. Although hurt badly at Arsuf, the Muslims were far from beaten.

Saladin's resistance surprised and troubled Richard. The sultan put up a good fight when cornered. Retaking the Holy Land would not be as easy as Richard had thought. Yet pushing the Christians back into the sea proved more difficult than

Saladin had anticipated. Both men wondered if now might not be a good time to talk. Richard moved first, and cautiously opened negotiations with the Muslims. The English king and the sultan feted and graciously bestowed gifts on each other's emissaries. Saladin treated Richard's ambassadors to lavish feasts at which they sampled Syrian and Egyptian delicacies while reclining on expensive carpets and ornate cushions. Richard, not to be outdone, actually knighted Saladin's grandson with his own royal sword! Notwithstanding all the pleasantries, the negotiations collapsed. Neither side was willing to compromise just yet.

STALEMATE

With peace through discussion no longer a possibility, the Muslims and crusaders turned back to war. Richard, after surveying the ruins of Ascalon and cursing his bad fortune, resigned himself to a siege and marched on Jerusalem. Soon, despite the best efforts of his Muslim adversaries, Richard stood within striking distance of the city. The king's forward elements claimed that they could even make out the skyline of Jerusalem glittering in the distance. Richard, however, was a long way from his supply ships out at sea and his position was dangerously exposed. He did not want to retreat, but each step forward took his army closer to what could be a devastating defeat. The Muslims no doubt would defend Jerusalem fanatically, making a direct assault suicidal, but logistics and the easily deflated morale of medieval soldiers argued against a long, exhausting siege. So, there he sat—too far from Jerusalem to draw the Muslims out of their shell, too far from the coast to wait forever.

Saladin, for his part, fretted just as much if not more than Richard did. Sitting like a dispirited lion in a cage, the sultan mourned the loss of Ascalon and tortured himself with questions. Demoralized and pessimistic, he worried about everything. Who would follow him after the multiple, ignominious defeats he had suffered? What could he do to repair his reputation? How could a sultan so averse to sieges successfully withstand one as powerful as Richard seemed sure to wrap around Jerusalem? His commanders only made things worse, challenging every decision Saladin made—especially the one to defend Jerusalem in the first place. After the disappointment of Acre, the emirs showed little stomach for a protracted stay within Jerusalem's walls. They could almost feel the pounding of the stones Richard's mangonels would throw, hear the whistle of crossbow bolts and the creaking of the siege towers, while the ominous thud of battering rams echoed in their heads. All this, while the food supplies from Egypt dwindled and the relief troops from Syria evaporated. Everyone could see that the same dire inevitabilities haunted Saladin. His face showed so much weariness and apprehension that a servant said, "Your highness is weighed down with anxiety and your soul is overburdened with care. . . . You can only turn to God Almighty." The next move would be either Allah's or Richard's.

WAR AND
PEACE

Saladin resigned himself to a siege of Jerusalem. The crusaders had everything they wanted except for the Holy City, and Saladin knew he would have to make his stand there. The sultan ordered that the city walls be reinforced and that springs within a radius of two miles be poisoned. If the outlying villages were deserted, the crops destroyed, and the water made undrinkable, Richard might come but he surely could not stay very long. Saladin would make the crusaders' visit to Jerusalem as difficult as humanly possible.

Yet he never put his faith in the works of men alone. Saladin prayed frequently and fervently, seeking solace in the comforting verses of the Koran. He reflected deeply on his faults and failings; all his mistakes came back to him. Saladin especially reproached himself for not yet having made the *hajj,* or journey to Mecca, that Allah required of all Muslims as one of the Five Pillars of Islam. Much worse than his spiritual doubts was the nagging feeling that he was

Saladin made a stand at Jerusalem, knowing that he and his army would have to dig in to defend the city. However, some of his lieutenants thought that militarily, this would not be the best option, and their constant second-guessing plagued Saladin.

losing control of events. Saladin sensed that Richard's agenda, rather than his own, would determine the next Muslim move.

Despite all this, Saladin still had to provide for the defense of Jerusalem; this he was resolved to do. But everyone did not share Saladin's convictions. Many of his emirs disagreed with him. Why defend Jerusalem? Would it not make better military sense to abandon the city and concentrate on destroying the crusader army in the field? How could a man, haunted by the ghosts of Alexandria, they wondered, conduct a successful defense under siege conditions? The most penetrating questions and strongest objections came surprisingly from Saladin's trusted mamluks. These most loyal and skilled fighters, an aide reported to Saladin, complained "about the plan for a siege." They did not approve of "us shutting ourselves up within the city." The mamluk commanders feared that their men would "surely meet the same fate as the garrison at Acre. In the meantime all the Muslim land will fall into the hands of the enemy." The mamluks concluded that it was better to lose Jerusalem than the jihad. "Islam can be protected without the Holy City!" they protested.

While Saladin suffered through countless sessions at which such arguments were raised, Richard positioned his army at Beit Nuba, within striking distance of Jerusalem. The leading edge of his column inched closer and closer to the city, skirmishing with Muslim patrols and scouting Muslim defensive works as they advanced. Saladin steeled himself for the fight ahead and asked God's blessing. He prayed for a miracle, and got one.

Richard had stopped. Saladin, it seemed, had not been alone in his misgivings about a siege. Richard had power enough to attack and perhaps take Jerusalem, but he did not possess the resources to camp outside its walls for months or maybe years. The luxury of time he had enjoyed at Acre no longer existed. Drinkable water was scarce, his food supply limited, and the morale of his men low. Long sieges were never an attractive option in medieval warfare. Richard's crusaders could look forward to hunger, thirst, disease, discomfort, and boredom. Sieges meant years away from home and family, during which time the ardor for conquest would surely wane. Saladin's men, everyone knew, would fight fiercely and offer dogged resistance. After so much hard combat, no one welcomed a bloody, prolonged struggle for Jerusalem.

Richard had personal problems as well. The king knew that his brother, John, was scheming at home in England. Family ties meant nothing to John; he wanted power for himself. How long before he moved to depose Richard and seize the throne? By early 1192, Richard realized that he had dangerous enemies before and behind him. The royal chancellor confirmed the king's suspicions. He wrote a letter to Richard in which he advised him to leave Palestine immediately and return to England on "wings of the wind." If he lingered too long in front of Jerusalem's walls, Richard stood a good chance of becoming a king without a kingdom.

Saladin had proven to be a clever and resourceful opponent. Try as he might, Richard could only deal out setbacks rather than conclusive defeats to the sultan. The king, in fact, began to despair of ever prevailing over his cagey foe. To his commanders, Richard expressed his foreboding:

> Wherever our army goes, Saladin knows our plan, the course we plan to follow, the number of our force. We are far distant from the coast. . . . Moreover, the perimeter of Jerusalem is long and its walls are thick and strong. It would take a great number of our soldiers to breach these walls. Who then would protect our supply lines? No one. These supply trains would be destroyed one and all. . . . I deem it wrong to rush rashly forward. We are ignorant of the narrow roads and defiles between here and Jerusalem. If we knew more, we might safely proceed, but we do not.

Richard had never before voiced such concerns. He had always exuded confidence; now, the great king sat frozen in ambivalence. Such was not the case with Richard's French allies. They exploded in a fit of indignation and outright contempt for the Lionheart who now lay paralyzed by indecision. "We left our own country only for the sake of the Holy City," they thundered, "and we will not return until we have taken it!" But Richard remained immobile and impassive. He preferred a swift return home to a slow siege of Jerusalem. Quarrels immediately broke out among the crusaders. Knights hurled accusations of cowardice at each other. Paralyzed by apprehension and disagreement, Richard's commanders could do little more than deflect blame and wonder why they ever came to Palestine. Above the din, Richard called for peace talks.

Weariness bore down heavier than any armor on both Richard and Saladin. Yet the men retained the dignity and presence of mind required of a king and a sultan. They longed for peace, but refused to pay for it with their honor. Richard opened the negotiations by stating his demands—he wanted to rebuild and keep Ascalon and receive a guarantee of free passage for Christians to the holy places in Jerusalem. The city itself the Muslims could keep.

Saladin countered with his demand for either the return of Ascalon or a promise that it would remain a neutral heap of rubble. Beyond that, Saladin consented to keeping Jerusalem open to Christian pilgrims. The sultan took his time in responding to Richard's offer, so much so that the king unexpectedly broke off the talks and retired to Acre. Saladin was a shrewd bargaining partner, and Richard could not afford to sit at Beit Nuba forever. Better, he thought, to pull back and give matters some time to develop.

DISGRACE AT JAFFA

Saladin quickly withdrew his offer and jumped at the chance to gain the initiative once again in the war. With Richard far away in Acre, southern Palestine would be ripe for the taking. The sultan could at once repair the damage done to his prestige and authority and give new impetus to the jihad. Saladin sent out an urgent call for reinforcements. Damascus, responding to his plea, rushed Kurdish and Turkish troops to Jerusalem.

As soon as the Syrian contingent joined his army, Saladin marched. His immediate target was the coastal city of Jaffa. The Muslims made quick work of Jaffa's defenders and then went

Saladin's army, assisted by reinforcements from Damascus, took over the city of Jaffa and the soldiers looted as much as they could, despite Saladin's objections. To add insult to injury, an attack by Richard involving an army that had far fewer soldiers than Saladin's actually defeated the Muslim fighters, and Richard took Jaffa and began negotiations with Saladin.

on a looting spree. Although Saladin had ordered otherwise, the Muslim soldiers carried off anything and everything of value. When the sultan tried to intervene, fighting broke out. Chaos erupted as Turks and Kurds fought against Saladin's mamluk guard. Saladin, impotent on the sidelines, was treated to the disgraceful sight of Islamic warriors struggling over gold chalices, fine garments, and livestock. What a disappointment it must have been to watch soldiers of Allah not only acting like common thieves, but also fighting amongst themselves in the middle of a jihad. Saladin had known intra-Muslim conflict before; he remembered Mosul and Aleppo. But principles had been involved then, political disagreements, disputes over legitimate authority. This was sheer greed. To make matters worse, Saladin received word that Richard was on his way.

Saladin commanded around 60,000 men at Jaffa; Richard confronted him initially with only 3,000 crusaders and three horses. The English king must have seemed crazy, or at least suicidal. Even more startling was the fact that Richard chose to lead personally the attack on Saladin's vastly superior force. This should have been the day Saladin had always dreamed of. He had his chance to crush the Franks once and for all.

Instead, Saladin's dream turned into a nightmare. The crusaders launched an audacious frontal assault on Saladin's line and quickly dispersed the Muslims. The ferocity of Richard's charge caught the Muslims by surprise and threw them into a panic. Before the emirs could stabilize their front and rally their men, a general rout began. Saladin stood dumbfounded as all around him swirled defeated soldiers running here and there, anywhere to escape the onrushing crusaders. Muslims dropped their weapons and fled the field as Saladin watched in shocked disbelief and disgust. Jaffa turned out to be a fiasco—Saladin had lost the city and his army. Peace talks began again soon afterward.

Richard, triumphant but feeling the long arm of his brother's betrayal in England, made extravagant offers to Saladin. Leave Jaffa and Ascalon unmolested, Richard proposed, and he would give Saladin a command in his service. Richard suggested that Saladin become one of his commanders, and he even promised to assign English soldiers to serve under the sultan and do his bidding.

Although flattered, Saladin still refused. Ascalon was the sticking point. "It is absolutely impossible for us to give up

Ascalon," Saladin wrote. He confided to Richard that accepting the English king's terms would imply nothing less than the failure of the jihad. He could weather defeats in battle, but declare the jihad a failure? This Saladin could not do. He was the "well-being of Islam"; losing the holy war would mean losing the very purpose of his life. "I am an old man now," Saladin said, "I have no longer desires for the pleasures of this world." Paraphrasing the Koran (3:13), Saladin concluded by saying, "I will not cease therefore until God grants victory to whom he will." The holy struggle would go on.

Saladin braced himself and ordered renewed hostilities. The Muslim war machine began to creep forward but soon stalled. Saladin's men moved reluctantly at first, then not at all. Next came total disobedience and outright mutiny. The men simply refused to fight. Saladin's army, the pride of Islam, the sword of Allah, had had enough. Whether the sultan liked it or not, the jihad was over. Nothing more could be done. Saladin's proud heart broke. The son of Ayyub had failed to retake the Holy Land. Yet Saladin had accomplished so much, had realized so many dreams. The little Kurdish boy had risen to become the Sultan of Syria and Egypt. He had unified Islam as no one had done since the days of the Prophet Muhammad himself. His father and Shirkuh could rest peacefully knowing they had given to Islam a great and pious leader. Saladin had come far from dusty little Tikrit; now he asked to speak with Richard once more.

THE TRUCE OF 1192

Exhausted and feeling the ill effects of one too many battles, Richard and Saladin swiftly came to an agreement to end what historians remember as the Third Crusade. The combatants would begin observing a four-year truce on September 2, 1192. After the expiration of the truce, the war could begin anew, although both sides knew this clause was a fiction. Neither Saladin nor Richard foresaw any more fighting in their future,

After working out a truce, Richard sailed for England. Both Saladin and Richard had grown weary fighting each other. Richard also had to attend to his brother John's scheming for power in England, while Saladin's army had simply lost their fervor for the jihad.

at least against each other. The heart of the agreement lay in its distribution of power in the now quiet Palestine. Ascalon would be left in ruins and abandoned. As neutral ground, no army could claim it. Those cities then in crusader hands would remain so, and Saladin agreed to guarantee free Christian access to Jerusalem's shrines and churches. In return, the Muslims would keep Jerusalem and (what a relief to Saladin!) Richard would leave for England. Peace had come to the holy places of two great religions.

9

THE SULTAN'S LAST DAYS

Saladin settled into a new routine after the truce with Richard. He had spent more than twenty years at war, ignoring his family and denying himself the perquisites of power. The time had finally arrived to tend to the little details of his sultanate.

Saladin first set out to tour Palestine. He wanted to study more closely and perhaps appreciate better this arid, rocky, yet strangely beautiful land he had fought so hard for. Jerusalem held a special attraction for him. Saladin had always viewed the Holy City through the distorted prism of military strategy. But Jerusalem was much more than a point on the map to be secured against the enemies of Allah. It was a living city that buzzed with the ordinary and extraordinary activities of urban society. Saladin loved visiting the Muslim shrines and mosques. He felt a little bit closer to God standing before the Dome of the Rock or losing himself in prayer within the walls of the al-Aqsa. Jerusalem could draw a faithful man in and calm his soul, and Saladin felt this.

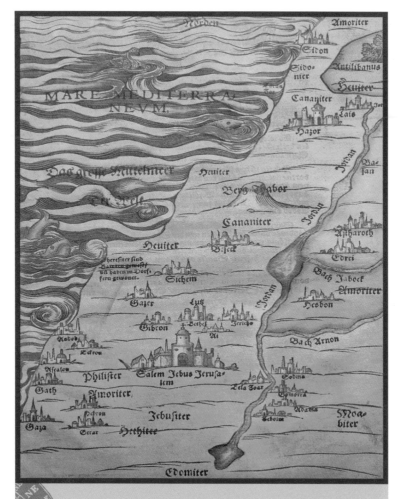

An early map of Palestine. Under the conditions of the truce with Richard, Saladin had agreed to allow Christians access to their places of worship in Jerusalem. Additionally, he founded a college and a hospital for the city before leaving for Damascus.

He also well understood the irresistible attraction the city held for Christian pilgrims. As with much else in his life, Saladin maintained contradictory views on the Christians he had labored unsuccessfully to expel from Palestine. On the one hand, they were infidels who had defiled the land of the

Prophet with their disbelief and refusal to hear the word of Allah. On the other, these were what the Koran called "People of the Book," God's children who had somehow gone astray. The Christians shared the Old Testament with Muslims and had to be considered in light of that fact. Saladin also admired the fiery devotion of men and women willing to travel over such great distances and suffer extreme hardships simply to stand in symbolic proximity to their Lord Jesus. Saladin pitied the Christians for their rejection of Muhammad, but respected them for their all-consuming faith. While in Jerusalem, Saladin made it a point to greet Christian pilgrims personally, treating them to generous helpings of his customary warmth and grace.

To the Muslim inhabitants of the city, Saladin dedicated his efforts to repair the physical and spiritual harm done by almost a century of war. Public works became a priority. Allah's people in Jerusalem, Saladin believed, deserved the best that any devout Muslim sultan had to offer. Before leaving for Damascus, he used his own money to establish a new hospital and college in the city. Jerusalem's citizens delighted in the overwhelming generosity of a man who cared as much for their minds and bodies in peace as he had worried over their defense in war.

The trip to Damascus was not easy. The long years of fighting and privation had left Saladin prematurely aged. He felt exhausted and his body ached with the cruel reminders of every day spent in battle. Life in the field had been hard on him; physical pain became his constant companion. Saladin had fought his way from the mountains of Syria to the banks of the Nile; now the old soldier longed for the simple pleasures of retirement, a longing that hastened his way home. Once there, Saladin spent his days relaxing, playing with his many grandchildren, and recounting, for all who would listen, tales of his years of service to Islam. He enjoyed his harem of wives, ate well, and savored the bliss of untroubled rest.

Still, Saladin knew that his present tranquility occupied the last stage in his life's journey. Old age heralded death, and he did not have long to prepare for his succession. Urgently, he called his sons together to make arrangements for a smooth and bloodless transition of power after his death. Saladin organized extended hunting trips in order to heal old wounds and erase festering resentments among his sons. He worked to bring unity to the ruling house so the Ayyubid dynasty could forge ahead without him. To his sons al-Zaher and al-Afdal, the sultan directed most of his advice and admonitions. He counseled the young men to remember where their obligations lay. Saladin warned them to guard against the domestic conflicts that could easily tear apart his painstakingly built but still fragile dynasty. "Beware of bloodshed," Saladin cautioned. "Trust not in that. Spilt blood never sleeps." Most importantly, Saladin advised, do not forget the common Muslims when thinking about politics: "Win the hearts of your people . . . and of your emirs and ministers. Such position as I have was won by gentleness and conciliation." Saladin recognized that clumsiness and miscalculation could undo a lifetime's labor. His sons were young and hotheaded. Saladin did not want his beloved Islam to suffer for their immaturity.

SALADIN'S FINAL CAMPAIGN

Saladin did indeed worry—about his sons, about the unity of Islam, about the Christian menace that still hovered over Palestine. Perhaps it was the stress of these cares that Saladin's attendants noted as they followed the sultan through his last days. After the reunion with his sons, people began to comment on the sultan's peculiar and troubling behavior.

His closest advisers noticed subtle but undeniable changes in Saladin. The dazed look in his eyes and an uncharacteristic forgetfulness concerned them greatly. On one particularly dreary, raw day, Saladin rode out to greet pilgrims returning from Mecca without first donning the thick padded tunic he always wore. The sultan had never forgotten it before, and his aides took the oversight as a bad omen. The next morning, Saladin felt a bit weak, then he began to shiver. His head hurt

Before dying, Saladin sought to ensure a smooth transition of power to his sons and among his political allies. He imparted advice to his sons al-Zaher and al-Afdal, hoping that they would mature enough to lead while properly handling the political and ideological differences of the Muslim empire.

and was warm to the touch. Taking to his bed, Saladin was sure that some rest would take care of things. But the fever worsened. He ate little at first, then nothing at all. The court physician could only call for Saladin's sons and prepare for the inevitable. Saladin's brother, al-Adil, accompanied the boys and with them began the ancient Muslim political ritual of playing for position among dynastic successors. Emirs had to be sounded out, alliances made, deals cut, and the possibility of war considered.

As the waters of competition and intrigue began to churn around him, Saladin prayed and reflected. Despite his illness, Saladin retained the good humor and gentle nature that war had often eclipsed but never entirely effaced. At one point, as his fever raged, Saladin cried out for water. The first glass brought to him was too warm; the second was too cold. Under similar conditions, most sultans would have summarily condemned to an excruciating death any servant unfortunate enough not to know what lukewarm meant. But Saladin simply sighed and smiling softly at the man said, "Perhaps there is no one who can make the water of the right temperature."

Saladin knew his time on this earth had come to an end. He summoned a trusted imam to his bedside to share his final moments with him. Together they read from the Koran. Saladin always sought refuge and reassurance in the Koran; now he listened attentively as the imam spoke to him of the comforts of heaven. Saladin's breaths grew shallow and his eyes fluttered. He loved life, but part of him wanted to let go. The Koran eased his tired soul and reconciled him to death. Speaking softly, the imam arrived at one of Saladin's favorite passages. He leaned close to the sultan and read, "He is the God than whom there is no other God; who knows the unseen and the visible." Saladin's eyes flashed their brilliance one last time. He smiled gently and whispered, "It is true." Al-Malik al-Nasir Salah al-Din Yusef ibn Ayyub died quietly at age 55 on March 4, 1193.

10

REMEMBERING SALADIN

Shortly after Saladin's death, a Muslim writer said that the sultan "was the ornament and admiration of the world." Indeed he was, at least for the Muslims he united and led. Saladin possessed qualities superior to those of any Muslim leader either before or after him. His sons never even came close to matching the heights of power and influence Saladin attained. To be sure, the Ayyubid dynasty he founded survived him by almost eighty years, but his sons played only minor roles in its history. Al-Afdal's brief tenure proved stormy as he dealt with suspicious brothers and a grasping uncle.

Arguably, Saladin's most effective successor was his brother Saif al-Din al-Adil. Al-Adil ruled from 1200 to 1218 and, after the tumult of al-Afdal's reign, restored a modicum of unity and order in Saladin's former realm. But nothing could prevent the slow decline of the Ayyubids. By the last third of the 13th century, their

While his successors were unable to maintain the Ayubbid dynasty's glories during his lifetime, Saladin will still be remembered as one of the greatest Muslim leaders of history, who united many different factions to fight the European crusaders. Unfortunately, some modern Muslims have taken Saladin's definition of jihad for their own purposes.

empire, so carefully and painstakingly crafted by Saladin, collapsed under the weight of repeated Mongol invasions and the rise of Mamluk Egypt.

A mournful Islam entombed the great sultan in Damascus's central citadel. Three years later, Saladin's body was removed and interred in a small domed mausoleum in the heart of the city where he grew up. He rests in this simple tomb today. That Saladin had anywhere at all to rest is surprising, considering the fact that he died penniless. He had given away all of his wealth to friends and people in need. The money for his funeral had to be borrowed. Saladin, without hesitation, did as the Koran commanded and disbursed all of his "wealth out of love for God . . . with a pure heart, seeking the way of God" (Koran, 2:177; 30:39). Undeniably, he gave his heart, soul, and life to his faith rather than earthly gain. Saladin asked nothing of this life but the opportunity to serve humbly his God as knew Him. He left little behind except for a legacy tied forever to the concept of jihad.

In her book *Holy War,* Karen Armstrong argues that the Crusades resulted in the creation of a new vocabulary for the conversation between Islam and Christianity. During the Crusades, Armstrong contends, these religions began to define one another in exclusive terms. Rather than recognizing the differences between Muslims and Christians as those one would expect to find between "cousins," especially when they are jostling for the same living space, people came to understand their religious dissimilarities as evidence of innate hostility. Put another way, the wars of the 12th and 13th centuries produced a new interpretive framework within which Islam and Christianity were not simply variants on the same theme, but unalterable and irreconcilable opposites. A model emerged in which unavoidable conflict between these extremes played a central role. Today, Armstrong concludes, Muslims and Christians find each other mutually incomprehensible and fundamentally threatening, and the Crusades are to blame.

The rhetoric employed by men such as Urban II—and, indeed, Saladin—artificially widened the gulf between the two great faiths and transformed conflicts with essentially geographic and political roots into wars for religious survival.

The Crusades, in other words, inaugurated a new discourse based on irrational fear, suspicion, and violence, built around non-negotiable theological assumptions. These were not simply wars anymore; they were titanic struggles between the forces of good and evil. At stake was nothing less than the ultimate triumph of God's chosen people—whoever they might be. It is through this distorted lens that Saladin's real legacy must be viewed.

Saladin defined his conflict with Christianity in terms of the Koranic principle of jihad, a word that today is synonymous with holy war. Jihad, however, does not translate into English literally as "holy war." Rather, it implies a more general struggle to insulate oneself against sin, doubt, and temptation, while striving to create a community of Believers. It does not necessarily mean a physical conflict with a specific, readily identifiable group or person. Jihad involves wrestling with evil influences, not killing evil people. Indeed, the Koran never equates jihad exclusively with violence; it merely asks of Muslims that they "strive in the way of God with a service worthy of him" (Koran, 22:78).

It is true that Muhammad had thought of his war against pagan Mecca (622–630) as a holy war, but he merely sought to end the city's resistance to the word of God. Muhammad wanted the Meccans to open their eyes and accept Allah. In the final analysis, the Meccan clans were Arabs, and, as such, he hoped to welcome them into the community of the faithful. His was not a war of irreconcilable opposites. Zengi and Nur al-Din used the term jihad during their clashes with the Franks, but they employed the word either as a powerful rallying cry or as a way to shame reticent Muslims into supporting policies of expansion put into place by the Zengid rulers of Syria. Neither Zengi nor Nur al-Din seriously used jihad to imply some sort of cosmic battle between Believers and infidels. Their objectives were firmly rooted in the worldly issues of the day.

Saladin, however, invoked the concept of jihad in a novel way. He linked jihad organically with the idea of a war between utterly antagonistic religious opposites. He set Islam and Christianity clearly against each other as political, social, cultural, and, above all, religious enemies. Christians posed a direct threat to Islam, Saladin believed, simply because they held beliefs that denied the supremacy of Allah. Thus, he reshaped the notion of jihad into a weapon against what he saw as a completely alien worldview that could never harmonize with his own. The followers of Christ were and would forever remain infidels. Saladin's contest with Christianity, then, was neither for the expansion of the Muslim community, nor was it a cynical effort to improve his geopolitical position; he truly saw his jihad as a holy war. As such, he felt compelled to cleanse Palestine of Christians in order to free Allah's faithful from the pollution of the infidels' presence.

Saladin's inner struggle to prove himself and his devotion in the eyes of God, a primary motive force since his boyhood, became externalized through his repackaging of the jihad. Saladin, for all his learning and compassion, envisaged a perpetual jihad against Christendom. Coexistence, even toleration, might be possible, but Christians would always be the enemy. Saladin tied jihad inextricably to the notion of an anti-Christian and later anti-Western holy war. He never could have anticipated the long-term consequences of this for his treasured Islam.

As Armstrong points out in her book, modern Islam is commonly miscast as a "religion of the sword." Although Islam is neither more nor less inherently violence-prone than any other religion, many people think of it as a warrior faith. There is a lingering misperception of Islam as an inordinately aggressive religion within which violence, specifically the Saladin-style jihad, plays an integral part. Television news-casts in Europe and North America deliver unsettling images

Saladin's tomb in a domed mausoleum (at left) in Damascus. The money for Saladin's funeral had to be borrowed, as he had given all of his money away to those less fortunate.

of death and destruction into living rooms seemingly every evening. People see the twisted wreckage of cars and buses, shattered buildings, and torn bodies, and are told it is all a consequence of jihad. Pictures are beamed in of children carrying automatic rifles and chanting bloodcurdling slogans and everything is attributed to a fanatical obsession with jihad. Skyscrapers explode and collapse before the television audience's eyes, and we are told it is because some Muslim in some faraway land declared a jihad against the infidels. In each case, the jihad in question represents a perversion of the Koran and a sad misreading of the Koranic message that Saladin espoused. Yet it was the notion of jihad embedded in this message that Saladin changed so radically. He, of course, never would have countenanced terrorism — everything about him would have argued against it. As he told his sons, spilled blood, especially innocent blood, never rested. Saladin could be a fierce warrior, but indiscriminate killing and senseless destruction always caused him great sorrow. And yet, the modern interpretation of jihad is a lethal distillation of his vision of holy war. However unintentionally, Saladin helped release the forces that today cast such a dark pall over Islam.

Saladin's legacy, then, lies neither in his devotion to God, nor in his apparently limitless compassion, nor in his legendary generosity. The world does not remember him for the copious tears he shed so readily for widows and orphans, nor does his name conjure up images of the hospitals and colleges he founded with his own money. Saladin's good nature and good humor are lost in the mists of time. Instead, history remembers him as the sultan who declared holy war against all Christianity. Saladin emerges unjustly but understandably as the architect of the jihad we know all too well. Yet the struggle, the jihad that Saladin really fought, took place in his own heart. Torn between the purity of faith and the impurity of the material world, Saladin projected his own anxieties outward. Saladin transformed the ongoing conflict between Islam and Christianity into far more than a struggle for temporal power between religious systems. None of the many mistakes he made seems so serious or unforgivable as this.

Saladin's shortcomings, though, were those of a man striving to transcend this life and to better serve the God he loved. He hoped that his flawed life would be acceptable to Allah and that his sins, many and enduring as they were, would ultimately be forgiven. The Kurdish boy who grew up to become the Sultan of Islam could take comfort from the Koran one final time in his eternal rest—"Surely those who believe and those who leave their homes and fight in the way of God, may hope for His benevolence, for God is forgiving and kind" (Koran, 2:218).

1096–1099   The First Crusade is fought and leads to the capture of Jerusalem by the Christians in 1099.

1138   Saladin is born.

1144   Imad al-Din Zengi conquers the Christian-controlled County of Edessa.

1146   Zengi is assassinated; his son Nur al-Din succeeds him.

1147–1149   The Second Crusade is fought. The Crusaders fail to take Damascus.

1152   The young Saladin goes to study under his uncle Shirkuh at Aleppo.

1154   Saladin's father, Ayyub, paves the way for his son's political career by convincing Damascus to ally itself with Nur al-Din.

1156   At age 18, Saladin rejoins his father in Damascus.

1164–1168   Saladin accompanies Shirkuh on several campaigns in Egypt, including defending the city of Alexandria during a siege by the Franks.

1169   Saladin becomes vizier of Egypt.

1171   The last Fatimid caliph dies. Saladin assumes control of Egypt.

1174   Nur al-Din dies. Saladin marches on Damascus and takes power in Syria. The caliph in Baghdad proclaims Saladin to be the sultan of Syria and Egypt.

1174–1186   Saladin consolidates his power through a series of battles against rebellious cities, chief among them Mosul and Aleppo.

1187   Saladin invades Palestine and defeats the Frankish armies led by Guy of Jerusalem and Raymond of Tripoli at Hattin. He moves on to capture Jerusalem that same year.

1188   Saladin's Palestinian campaign gives him all of the important strong points in the region except for Tripoli, Tyre, and the fortress at Krak des Chevaliers.

1188–1191 The siege of the Muslim city of Acre ends in Saladin's greatest defeat against English king Richard the Lionheart.

1192 Richard and Saladin agree to a truce that requires them to share control over the Holy Land.

1193 Saladin dies at age 55.

Al-Qur'ân. Trans. Ahmed Ali. Princeton, New Jersey: Princeton University Press, 1994.

Armstrong, Karen. *Holy War: The Crusades and Their Impact on Today's World.* New York: Anchor Books, 1988.

————. *Islam: A Short History.* New York: The Modern Library, 2000.

Armstrong, Karen. *Muhammad: A Biography of the Prophet.* San Francisco: HarperSanFrancisco, 1992.

Dupuy, R. Ernest and Trevor Dupuy, eds. *The Encyclopedia of Military History,* 2nd ed. New York: Harper & Row, 1986.

Lyons, Malcolm Cameron and D. E. P. Jackson. *Saladin: The Politics of Holy War.* London: Cambridge University Press, 1982.

Newby, P. H. *Saladin in His Time.* London: Phoenix Press, 1983.

Nicolle, David. *Saladin and the Saracens.* Illus. Angus McBride. Edited by Martin Windrow. Men-At-Arms, no. 171. Oxford, England: Osprey Publishing, 1986.

Nicolle, David. *Saracen Faris, AD 1050–1250.* Illus. Christa Hook. Edited by Martin Windrow. Men-At-Arms, no. 10. Oxford, England: Osprey Publishing, 1994.

Oldenbourg, Zoé. *The Crusades.* Trans. Amy Carter. London: Weidenfeld and Nicolsen, 1966.

Regan, Geoffrey. *Lionhearts: Richard I, Saladin, and the Era of the Third Crusade.* New York: Walker and Company, 1998.

Reston, James Jr. *Warriors of God: Richard the Lionheart and Saladin in the Third Crusade.* New York: Doubleday, 2001.

Stearns, Peter, ed. *The Encyclopedia of World History,* 6th ed. Boston: Houghton Mifflin Company, 2001.

Wise, Terence. *Armies of the Crusades.* Illus. G. A. Embleton. Edited by Martin Windrow. Men-At-Arms, no. 75. Oxford, England: Osprey Publishing, 1978.

Firestone, Reuven. *Jihad: The Origin of Holy War in Islam.* New York: Oxford University Press, 1999.

Gabrieli, Francesco, ed. *Arab Historians of the Crusades.* Trans. Francesco Gabrieli. Berkeley: University of California Press, 1969.

Hillenbrand, Carole. *The Crusades: Islamic Perspectives.* London: Routledge, 2000.

Maalouf, Amin and Jon Rothschild. *The Crusades Through Arab Eyes.* New York: Schocken Books, 1984.

Madden, Thomas F. *A Concise History of the Crusades.* Lanham, Maryland: Rowman and Littlefield, 1999.

Riley-Smith, Jonathan. *The Crusades: A Short History.* New Haven: Yale University Press, 1990.

Saladin Homepage
http://www.acsamman.edu.jo/~ms/crusades/saladin/saladin.html

Encyclopedia of the Orient
http://lexicorient.com/cgi-bin/eo-direct-frame.pl?http://i-cias.com/e.o/saladin.htm

page:

2:	Leonard de Selva/ Corbis	61:	Corbis
13:	Hulton Archive/Getty Images	65:	Bettmann/Corbis
18:	Archivo Iconographico, S.A./ Corbis	68:	Hulton Archive/Getty Images
21:	Archivo Iconographico, S.A./ Corbis	71:	Gianni Dagli Orti/ Corbis
24:	Hulton Archive/Getty Images	75:	Hierophant Collection
29:	Hulton-Deutsch Collection/Corbis	78:	Historical Picture Archive/Corbis
32:	Archivo Iconographico, S.A./ Corbis	81:	Paul A. Souders/Corbis
36:	K.M. Westermann/Corbis	85:	Historical Picture Archive/Corbis
41:	Bettmann/Corbis	89:	Bettmann/Corbis
45:	Bettmann/Corbis	92:	David Rubinger/Corbis
50:	Richard T. Nowitz	98:	Bettmann/Corbis
53:	Historical Picture Archive/Corbis	101:	Hulton Archive/Getty Images
57:	Michael Masan Historic Photographs/Corbis	105:	Corbis

Cover: Hierophant Collection
Frontis: SEF/Art Resource. NY

JOHN DAVENPORT holds a Ph.D. from the University of Connecticut and currently teaches at St. Raymond School in Menlo Park, California. He lives in San Carlos, California, with his wife, Jennifer, and his two sons, William and Andrew.

ARTHUR M. SCHLESINGER JR. is the leading American historian of our time. He won the Pulitzer Prize for his book *The Age of Jackson* (1945) and again for a chronicle of the Kennedy administration, *A Thousand Days* (1965), which also won the National Book Award. Professor Schlesinger is the Albert Schweitzer Professor of the Humanities at the City University of New York and has been involved in several other Chelsea House projects, including the series REVOLUTIONARY WAR LEADERS, COLONIAL LEADERS, and YOUR GOVERNMENT.